Mark Moses

The Municipal Financial Crisis

A Framework for Understanding and Fixing Government Budgeting

palgrave
macmillan

Mark Moses
California, USA

ISBN 978-3-030-87835-1 ISBN 978-3-030-87836-8 (eBook)
https://doi.org/10.1007/978-3-030-87836-8

Cover illustration: Venimo

This Palgrave Macmillan imprint is published by the registered company Springer Nature Switzerland AG
The registered company address is: Gewerbestrasse 11, 6330 Cham, Switzerland

The Municipal Financial Crisis

Acknowledgments

First, I would like to thank Jeff Britting, a long-time friend, who was prescient in seeing the potential for this project long before it could be called a project. Over dinner some fourteen years ago, Jeff suggested that I consider writing about my experiences in and perspective on local government. It took several years for that idea to gel and the past four to make it real. Jeff helped me navigate a new professional terrain. I am indebted to him for his unwavering personal and editorial support and for helping me articulate the value of government.

Also critical to this book was Don Watkins. Don, an accomplished author and communicator, took me on as a client during summer 2020 and taught me invaluable writing and communication skills during a formative period of this project. Don patiently coached me, reviewed my writing, and showed me a way to better thinking and clearer writing.

Another person whom I was fortunate to meet through this project is Marc Joffe. I have since become an admirer of Marc's journalism, and I appreciate the feedback he provided. I am also grateful to Marc for referring me to my publisher. I thank Patrick Peterson for introducing me to Marc and for his encouragement and useful book recommendations.

I would also like to thank Charles Berry for his edits to early drafts of the book and Maryallene Arsanto, Jeri Eagan, and Tracy Fuller for taking the time to read and comment on a late draft.

None of the aforementioned individuals weighed in on the final draft. Thus, the responsibility for the final content and formulations that follow are mine.

It has been a pleasure to work with the editing team and production team at Palgrave Macmillan. Everyone was amazingly supportive throughout the process.

Finally, thank you to all of the dedicated people in and around the local governments that I have worked with over the past few decades. You have enriched my life as well as the lives of those in your communities.

Contents

About the Author

Mark Moses has consulted California municipal governments in the areas of finance and administration since 2011. Also during that time, he served municipalities in finance director roles. Prior, he spent two decades working directly for local government in senior management positions. His early career included small businesses consulting and banking.

Mr. Moses holds a Master of Business Administration in Finance from Golden Gate University, San Francisco, and a Bachelor of Science in Industrial Engineering and Operations Research from the University of California, Berkeley.

List of Tables

1

Introduction

When I began working as a financial analyst in municipal government in the early 1990s, I imagined that my background and skills would be especially applicable to government organizations. In university, nearly a decade before, I studied industrial engineering, a subject in which principles developed in the manufacturing field can be used to improve productivity in service industries. Following graduation, I spent a decade in the private sector, working in the fields of banking and small business consulting. But the companies I worked for proved unstable and unpredictable. Over time, the prospect of working for municipal governments grew appealing. Surely such enduring organizations would welcome strategies to improve internal operations and service delivery. I anticipated a problem solver's paradise.

What I found was quite different.

The *stability* of municipal government institutions, at first enticing, did not provide any real opportunity for the continuous operational improvements I had envisioned. In fact, there were equally stable institutional forces that encouraged municipal governments to oppose operational improvements. I discovered that government organizations took on new obligations faster than such obligations could be met. And while the values of *continuous improvement* and *efficiency* were explicit goals of the municipalities for which I worked, the delivery of these goals failed. Each new budget was a reminder of this failure. Meanwhile, municipal governments were slipping further behind both operationally and financially. The financial signals were ominous.

M. Moses, *The Municipal Financial Crisis*,
https://doi.org/10.1007/978-3-030-87836-8_1

Today in the 2020s, the financial slippage I observed has become an enduring *municipal financial crisis.* Municipal government operations are not sustainable financially. The evidence keeps accumulating. Just consider: the $130 billion in federal relief to municipalities (a *bailout* if given to private corporations)[1]; the trend of rising municipal fees and taxes; the deteriorating public infrastructure; and the struggle of local governments to pay for employee retirement benefits. In addition to these signs, there is the ongoing degradation of well-established local services, such as municipal water (availability and quality), police patrol, and park maintenance. Meanwhile, municipalities—despite their financial shortfalls—are choosing to *expand* their scope of activity.

In my role of finance director in several mid-range California municipalities, I observed all of the above and more on a daily basis. This trend has reached its climax. Presently, the reliability and quality of local government services is jeopardized—and the economic and physical well-being of residents and local business owners, who depend upon those services, is threatened. Making matters worse, the situation has become accepted as routine—a routine now endangering life and property.

During my time in government finance, I searched for comprehensive studies of the unfolding crisis. However, I found only two books that addressed the growing municipal fiscal turmoil: *Reinventing Government* (1992), which presented a vision of an "entrepreneurial" government; and *The Price of Government* (2004), which built upon the earlier book and championed "Budgeting for Outcomes." Although these books inspired some positive changes, the results were temporary. Over time, I began to realize why. Neither of the books addressed and defined the essence of *what government is.* Thus, as much as these two books purported to disrupt and reinvent government operations, they merely perpetuated an unexamined *status quo.*

During the nearly two decades since the publication of *The Price of Government*, journalists have continued to document, at exhaustive length, such developments as municipal debt accumulation, pension obligations, and the political power of public employee unions. But this reporting, while often perceptive, lacks a broad, causal explanation for the current state of municipal finance and its implications for local government. The reporting amasses evidence of the crisis in concrete detail. But these journalists, as with the authors of the previously mentioned books, do not provide a higher level

[1] Kate Davidson, "Federal Covid-19 Aid Aims to Help Cities, States Avoid Cutting Jobs and Services," *The Wall Street Journal*, March 18, 2021, https://wsj.com/articles/federal-covid-19-aid-aims-to-help-cities-states-avoid-cutting-jobs-and-services-11616059802.

perspective on that detail. Thus, they do not provide a basis for any real, sustainable solutions.

In the past, as I walked the corridors of city hall, I often asked myself: with so much at stake, why were there no successful studies of the underlying causes of the financial crisis? And why did municipal officials—frontline eyewitnesses to the crisis and its negative consequences—fail to find fresh solutions? I saw the evidence of crisis growing around me; yet, despite the growing mound of detail, something about the approach of my colleagues was shrinking. Then something new occurred to me. My colleagues did not need a new set of facts in order to take action. They needed a different perspective on the known facts—a new *framework*.

After thirty years in municipal government finance, I realized that a traditional decision-making approach—now embedded firmly in the minds of municipal managers—was fundamentally responsible for the municipal financial crisis. Traditional municipal decision-making does not account for what government is, what it should be doing, or what clear principles should guide it. And yet such an approach was being used to both evaluate the crisis and resolve it. The approach failed with each new round of budgeting, leaving even the most accomplished city officials and policy experts floundering with little new to offer. It was time to consider a completely new framework for understanding and resolving the municipal financial crisis.

That is the goal of this book.

In Chapter 2, I present several manifestations of the municipal financial crisis and explain why a new framework is needed to resolve the crisis. In Chapter 3, I examine municipal budgeting and show why the traditional municipal budgeting process is ineffective. Then, in Chapter 4, I evaluate the two chief alternatives to traditional municipal budgeting: zero-base budgeting and performance budgeting, and I explain how these budgeting solutions reinforce the false decision-making approach that causes fiscal instability.

In Chapter 5, I examine the failure of municipal financial and economic analysis to ensure budget stability. Rather than prevent poor financial decisions, inadequate analysis in these areas provides justification for such decisions. In Chapter 6, I survey several prevalent financial remedies, failing conventions that are adopted out of sheer desperation. Then in Chapter 7, I begin presenting the new framework. First, I describe how I came to understand the value of city government. I then discuss the nature of city government, what it is, and what it is not. I also explain why effective budgeting requires an understanding of what government is.

In Chapter 8, building on an explicit understanding of what government is, I present a clear decision-making standard for determining what city government should do—one based on protecting individual judgment and autonomous action. This standard is contrasted with the inherently vague standard of "community interest" used in the traditional municipal approach. In Chapter 9, I apply the new perspective on the scope of government, coupled with the new decision-making standard, to municipal budgeting and derive a new approach, which I call *Budgeting for Scope*. The new approach is guided by the new standard, which delimits the government's scope of activity, thereby ensuring that local government is operationally and financially manageable. In Chapter 10, I discuss municipal officials' exciting opportunity to decide the financial and existential future of their cities through their response to this crisis. These leaders can ensure the efficacy of their operational and fiscal management for the sake of their residents, whose quality of life they will enhance in the process. In this chapter, I also present the consequences of sustaining the traditional decision-making approach.

This book is not a disinterested study of municipal government. It is based on my observations and experience that began in that financial analyst position three decades ago and continues today. In these chapters, I provide my account of municipal government, municipal management, and municipal finance. I do so in order to present how I reached the conclusions that I did about the municipal financial crisis and what it will take to solve it.

How many times have proposals to reshape government been criticized for their *political naïveté*? And how many times has this cast self-doubt on the quest for real solutions? Perhaps many. But I do not believe that mere politics—or self-doubt—explains why these solutions have proven ineffective. The better answer is that the solutions are not real. The depth of the financial mire we now find ourselves inhabiting is beyond fixing through practical politics—the real solution is framework changing, which means *philosophical*.

If we are going to fix municipal budgeting, we must examine what drives it, how decisions are made, and what characteristics fundamental to local government organizations shape the process. And that is only possible when you examine the framework responsible for not merely municipal budgeting, but the very purpose of government itself. *That* is what I undertake. The solutions that I present in this book begin a new discussion of the scope and range of government services, not their elimination. Government has a role to play, and it is not a begrudging role. Rather, it is an absolutely life-serving role that the honest on either side of the political aisle can affirm and accept. My goal in this book is to *integrate* the levels of discourse on the scope of local government, not just *raise* them. By combining knowledge of actual financial operations with a new, integrating framework and an actionable budgeting solution—we can take the first, long-overdue steps toward understanding, and resolving, the municipal financial crisis.

2

Cities in Crisis

There was an alleged exchange in the 1950s between golfing great Sam Snead and baseball legend Ted Williams regarding which sport is more challenging. Ted pointed out that a baseball batter must hit a ball moving unpredictably at speeds that can exceed 90 miles per hour and, therefore, must start his swing before he knows where the ball will be by the time it reaches him. In contrast, the golf ball is still, and a golfer can take as long as he wants to prepare for and execute his swing. Sam's unanswerable response was, "Ted, you don't have to go up in those stands and play your foul balls."

In contrast to institutions in the commercial and nonprofit sectors, municipalities must play their foul balls.

In every municipality where I have worked, I observed a management hampered by past decisions and indecision. I encountered computer systems only partially implemented, active contracts that no one understood, and unresolved property ownership. Often this unfinished business went back not simply years, but multiple decades. The weight of such unresolved issues made it difficult to move forward. Compounding matters were legacy labor provisions, failed commercial ventures, and the effects of a previous lax approach to financial reporting. The longer these issues remained, the less urgent they became. After all, the organizations were still standing.

In private industry, the impact of bad decisions and unfinished business is transitory. Organizations that make poor decisions quietly disappear, or their assets transpose elsewhere. The speed of business reduces the likelihood that a policy or directive will outlast its usefulness. Competition, mergers,

M. Moses, *The Municipal Financial Crisis*,
https://doi.org/10.1007/978-3-030-87836-8_2

acquisitions, divestitures, industry cycles, product cycles, and a more frequent rate of employee turnover ensure regular disruption and reinvention.

The average lifespan of modern corporations has been declining for decades. Meanwhile, municipalities are growing older. And the foul balls—or languishing, unresolved issues—are growing in number. Typically, local governments do not contemplate their demise. Disincorporation is rare. And municipal bankruptcy only offers relief from debt and other financial obligations, which leaves the organization, along with its unresolved practices and other baggage, intact.

The differences between working in a financially challenged, temporal organization and one considered to be everlasting are vast. I once prepared dozens of financial projections for a bank whose ability to survive the next 60 days was an ongoing question. Some of the bank's employees left for more stable or promising work environments, while others remained. Those who remained labored in an atmosphere of total uncertainty. I contrast that experience in the private sector with its equivalent in local government. In working for a financially troubled city, proving to everyone's satisfaction that the financial condition of the organization is in fact dire can take a year or more. In the meantime, there is rarely any urgency.

In the face of dire circumstances, business-as-usual operations and the consequences of past municipal decisions are significant drains on scarce financial resources. And while some jobs are at immediate risk, most employees are not worried. Vacations are neither canceled nor interrupted. Emergency city council and municipal board meetings are rare. This should not be surprising. The overwhelming majority of jobs will continue—and no one believes that the organization's survival is at stake. Cursed with seeming immortality, municipalities have an endless number of innings in which to play their foul balls.

The consequences of managing a perpetual organization are just one facet of the crisis. There are several others. There is rampant confusion regarding the nature of the crisis and how to describe it. Such confusion is worsened by disjointed municipal funding and spending dynamics, which make the financial problems appear intractable. Meanwhile, vague organizational missions and visions provide a weak basis for decision-making. This decision-making is further weakened by poor, unquestioned assumptions. All of these factors contribute to the current crisis in municipal budgeting. It is useful to understand all of them, if for no other reason than to help sort through the confusion. The most fundamental of these factors, and what I will be examining throughout, is the municipal decision-making approach.

Let us start with the confusion that surrounds a city's budget. When I was deeply involved in municipal budget development, I struggled to keep track of all of the assumptions, all of the issues, and all of the moving parts. I cannot imagine how any outside observer could make sense of the outcome of a municipal budget meeting. And to anyone relying on the local news, the coverage of such meetings must be mystifying. At first, stories break with announcements of budget deficits, portending doom. Within a matter of weeks the narrative shifts to the just-in-time resolution—a balanced budget. The deficit is forgotten. Then several months later, when the books are closed for the prior year, a budget surplus is revealed. No one asks for clarification, so the confusion persists. It is impossible to distinguish such uneventful sequences from those that foreshadow an actual financial collapse.

Most of those inside local government are likewise bewildered. How does city management convince labor union representatives that employee compensation needs to be restrained when, year after year, the city *somehow* manages to balance its budget? How does a city manager motivate a department head to reduce the scope of activity in her department when the finance director *somehow* finds a way to resolve budget shortfalls? In such an environment, why would the city reject *any* new program that fits however loosely with its goals?

Sadly, city officials—those empowered to direct the organization's activities—are as confused as everyone else. They do not know what to do. And they are not asking the questions that would bring them closer to a productive solution. Whether they think their organization's struggle to achieve financial stability is a new normal or an old normal, most city officials accept such ongoing struggle as the norm.

When searching for solutions, city officials struggle to name the problem. Is it a lack of control over salary costs? Is it the cost of open-ended (i.e., defined benefit) pension and retiree medical benefits? Is it the inability to improve the way services are delivered? Is it an unwillingness to terminate activities that should be shed, but are politically favored? Is it unrealistic expectations from the community? Is it inadequate accounting and financial reporting standards? Is it a matter of insufficient tax revenues or state distributions? I have heard all of these questions posed.

Many people outside local government (e.g., citizen groups, taxpayer organizations, think tanks, etc.) have given their answers to these questions. Most of these observers cannot fathom why local government finds operating within the organization's financial means to be elusive. But none of these groups have prompted noteworthy breakthroughs. I am sure that to such groups municipalities must seem impenetrable.

Municipal managers and industry consultants, those closest to the problem and with the greatest access to pertinent information, fare no better with these questions. Nor are they able to offer viable solutions. The prevalent municipal financial remedies do not lead to meaningful or sustained improvements to the organization's financial health. I know because I have tried them all.

In the course of applying the conventional financial remedies, I observed that most municipalities' problems are self-inflicted. Notwithstanding legal mandates, municipalities have a great deal of control over what they do and how they do it. Unfortunately, these organizations are rarely in touch with that control. I saw evidence of this detachment whenever I asked city staff two questions: Why does the city do this? and Why does the city do this in this manner? I was astonished by the hesitant answers to these questions. But more astonishing is that no one was embarrassed by their answers. It is completely acceptable to be uninformed about why the organization has undertaken something and why it does things the way it does. I could not accept this surrender to obliviousness. I needed to understand. If the problems are self-inflicted, then they are solvable.

I want to see the problems of local government finance solved, not simply to save the organizations as an end in itself, but to secure the elements of local government that we need to live our lives well. It is natural to think of local government in terms of one's last encounter—a water bill, a building permit, a business license, or an emergency service call. But when I think about how to save local government, I think about saving the elements that recognize our needs and protect us so we can plan our days, choose our careers, and live our lives. The remarkable things that we see and enjoy when we move about our cities, pursuing our own values, have only been built and preserved because we *can* move about our cities and pursue our values.

Missing from the conventional approach to municipal management is a way for officials to examine what local government does that is important to the human needs of residents and thriving of businesses and what it does that detracts from this aim. What things critical to residents' lives does municipal government enable, and what does it restrain? This distinction is vital to examining local government operationally and financially, planning the path forward, and reaffirming the ends of local government. Reaffirming the ends of local government is the topic that city officials should be discussing in city halls today—but it is a topic that no one places on the agenda.

If a local government does not know what it does in relation to the human needs of residents, how does it know when to intervene? And how does it know what goals to establish? Without clarity in these areas, how does it successfully design solutions to financial distress?

Local governments operate most comfortably when they are following familiar procedures and conducting business as usual. They treat the scope of what they do as settled, except when they are expanding that scope. These organizations act as though they have always been here, they have always been doing what they currently do, and they will always be doing it. Contrary to what is projected by their demeanor, the local government institutions we have today are new by historical standards. The formative decisions that set the scope of local government were made between the mid-1800s and early 1900s. And decisions regarding this scope—for better or worse—were shaped by the values and goals of those who were influential at the time. It is time now to evaluate which decisions were for better and which were for worse.

The first public police force was established in Boston, in 1838. Fifteen years later, the first city fire department was formed in Cincinnati. The public parks and recreation movements became active in the mid-to-late 1800s as industrialization shortened the workday. This resulted in the emergence of city parks, bath houses, and gymnasiums over the next several decades. The formation of public water and sewer utilities burgeoned during the late 1800s. Meanwhile, public works as a local government concern began modestly in the late 1800s and expanded over the next several decades with the paving of existing roads and the building of new roads. City land use planning and zoning emerged on both coasts in the early 1900s and were made portable by legislation championed by then Commerce Secretary Herbert Hoover.

Most people take the resulting scope of activity for granted, rarely reflecting upon the history. But I often wondered how former officials made decisions regarding the scope and range of municipal activity. Of course, no one can change these decisions. But we can—and I will—evaluate how elements underlying those decisions guide municipal officials' decisions today.

Until recently, it appeared unnecessary to examine municipal government history or the underlying decision-making approach. That is because the decades that followed the Great Depression were characterized by strong economic growth. Municipal financial crises were infrequent and low profile. Bankruptcy and dissolution were limited to small jurisdictions—e.g., hospital, water, and sanitation districts. New York City's near bankruptcy in 1975 and Cleveland's loan defaults in 1978 were notable but rare exceptions. The few city and county bankruptcies did not occur until decades later. And the first of these financial collapses were rooted in singular events, such as Orange County's investment losses (1994) and Desert Hot Springs' legal judgment (2001).

By the early 2000s, waning economic growth exposed the accumulation of municipal financial commitments as well as organizational inflexibility. The absence of major financial failures up to that time constituted only the *appearance* of financial stability and organizational adaptability. Beginning in 2008, the United States witnessed a geographically diverse succession of high-profile municipal bankruptcies that did not emerge from extraordinary events and circumstances: Vallejo, 2008; Jefferson County, 2011; Stockton 2012; San Bernardino, 2012; and Detroit, 2013. Then it struck me. Municipal governments are managing their way to financial failure.

Today, the struggle to meet debt obligations, satisfy employee retirement commitments, and maintain services threatens hundreds, if not thousands, of local governments nationwide. The cost to bring city streets, buildings, and other infrastructure into good repair is mounting, just as the count of retirees—for whose past work municipalities still pay—exceeds the count of current employees. As recently as a few years ago, it was extraordinary for a city official to declare a looming fiscal crisis. Such a public declaration was an admission of management failure, a strategy to game the labor negotiations process, or a sign that a rare municipal bankruptcy was imminent. Now, it is unremarkable for city officials to openly acknowledge financial despair.

The municipal bankruptcies since 2008—small in number—are proving ominous. But even if the incidence of formal bankruptcy and state takeovers remains small, such events do not constitute the only evidence of municipal failure. Avoiding insolvency by deferring maintenance, desperately selling assets, shifting costs to a future generation, relying on state or federal aid, and increasing taxes serially are tantamount to a management failure. Meanwhile, local officials cut back services not by design, but out of desperation. Then there are the many city governments that have fallen behind in their accounting, rendering them unable to report on their current financial condition.

An organization's approach to decision-making guides what it does. No one in the city could explain why the organization does what it does because no one thinks in those terms. No one questions the traditional approach or the earlier decisions. But if cities can manage their way into insolvency, they can manage their way out. They need a framework—a framework for understanding what now seems incomprehensible—a framework from which real solutions can emerge.

Deciding Where to Start

How can one be sure that "municipal financial crisis" does not overstate the problem facing local governments?

To answer this question, let us examine some municipal financial trends and key elements of municipal management.

Most cities meet each new period of economic slowdown without having recovered from the previous one. US cities had not fully recuperated from the dotcom crash of the early 2000s when, in 2007, the Great Recession emerged. Even the decade-long recovery that followed the Great Recession proved insufficient for many cities to survive the COVID-19 response without the 2021 federal aid package. To appreciate why municipalities lose ground with each successive recovery and what this means for effective municipal financial management, it is helpful to be familiar with the disjointed nature of the city funding, operating, and spending paradigm.

Revenues and resources. When I became acquainted with municipal finance, I was astonished to learn of the accidental nature of a city's revenues and other financial resources. In other settings that I had encountered, revenues bear a direct relationship to the value the organization provides via its products or services. Additional resources are provided by the organization's investors. Similarly, a charitable (as opposed to commercial) nonprofit organization must offer value through its activities that resonates with its donors. Regardless of whether these organizations are successful in fulfilling their respective missions, their revenues and resources have a clear tie to the demand for their offerings. This demand—expressed through revenues—shapes the activities of these organizations, including the ability to expand or the need to shrink. A for-profit organization responds to demand in the context of generating a return on investment, while a nonprofit must prioritize and scale its activities within the limitations of its donation sources.

In stark contrast, the primary basis for a city's tax revenues is historical, varying from state to state, from county to county, and from city to city. The major tax revenues include property tax, sales tax, business license, etc. These taxes are usually supplemented by distributions from the state. In some cases, cities have expanded their property and sales taxes with special taxes dedicated to a restricted use (e.g., library, parks, public safety, facility renovation, etc.). Notwithstanding a city council's intent and ballot declarations, these special taxes are not tied to the delivery of any specific array of municipal services. Even in cases in which a special tax is characterized as "buying 25 hours per month of library access" or "funding six additional police officers," there is no assurance that the tax revenue will always be sufficient to support the stated services.

The California local tax structure exemplifies how city revenues are detached from the cost of the organization's activities and commitments. The California state sales tax rate is 7.25%. Of this, 1% is given to incorporated cities. For example, a $100 taxable retail sale in a city yields the city government $1. A city with robust retail activity and a small population can receive several hundred dollars or more per resident annually, while a residential suburb lacking such commerce receives negligible amounts.

Meanwhile, the baseline property tax throughout California is 1% of the assessed value. Buying a new home for $500,000 will initially oblige the owner to pay an annual property tax of $5,000. The portion of the $5,000 that is distributed to the city is based upon the tax structure that happened to be in place more than forty years ago. Although there are historical reasons for this structure (e.g., previous tax decisions and negotiations with other municipal agencies), any tie to the cost of providing specified services lies in the distant past.

One consequence of this legacy methodology is that for merely *historical reasons*, one California city would receive nearly $1,700, or 33%, of the $5,000 annual property tax, while another would receive $1,250, or 25%, and many throughout the state would receive less than $500 (i.e., less than 10%) in this example.

Even in states in which cities have significant discretion in setting annual property tax rates (e.g., Minnesota, New Hampshire, and Tennessee), the tax rates are not bound by anything definitive. In such states, city officials set tax rates under a wide range of assumptions regarding the long-term cost of maintaining streets, buildings, and other municipal infrastructure. Annual adjustments appear to recalibrate the budget. In fact, such adjustments only propagate the detached nature of the organization's revenues.

When one considers the absence of a solid connection between a city's major revenues and resources and the cost of the activities in which a city is engaged, the disparate severity of financial pressure faced by cities is not surprising. I cannot conclude that a city that lacks financial desperation is truly stable. It may have assets that it can sell to keep the organization solvent. Or the city's revenues may be temporarily propped up by a spurt in development activity. Nor can I conclude that a city facing budget shortfalls is mismanaged. There can be legitimate financial challenges in a city with limited resources and a critical need for police and fire services.

Some consider the disconnect between local taxes and municipal services to be a positive feature of the system and not a bug. Under this view, it is desirable for a local government to have maximum flexibility in how it secures revenues and makes spending decisions. But my point is not that the disconnected nature of city tax revenues is an inherent problem. Rather, it is a factor that needs to be recognized when evaluating municipal finance and budgeting.

Organizational structure and staffing. A city's optimal organizational structure and staffing arrangement would be consistent with that which an informed, experienced city manager would freely design today. Unfortunately, such a design would be exceptional. City management encounters few opportunities to manage the organizational structure and staffing comprehensively.

When cities face financial pressure, they routinely leave vacant positions unfilled and encourage voluntary retirements as the preferred means of reducing staff. When these organizations lay off workers, labor contracts usually prescribe the process. As revenues recover, city management rebuilds the organization. Often, labor groups and some of the organization's managers advocate for a return to the earlier staffing structure. However, such a structure may not provide the best support to the organization's emergent needs. But changes to organizational structure require the city management to negotiate with labor groups over staffing levels and job descriptions that affect union membership levels and employee compensation. Such barriers to change make it more attractive for city management to work within the existing staffing structure than to reform it.

Even when pressure to revert to the previous staffing structure is mild, it is easier for management to reinstate a position that was suspended than to create a new one. Occasionally, a city manager can make an isolated strategic staffing change. But the organizational structure of cities is shaped mostly by the accident of unfilled positions of several years ago, layoff rules, employee decisions to retire, and old job descriptions.

Systems and methods of service delivery. To deliver local services, city management is faced with how to use city staff, which technology to adopt, and what procedures for staff to follow. The inflexibility of organizational design and staffing hampers management's ability to carry out anything more than simple, incremental improvements to service delivery methods. An organization cannot make significant changes to a system that relies heavily on employees without affecting those employees. One consequence of operating this way is that many cities utilize cutting-edge technology in high-profile areas such as police and fire operations, where demand for the best tools prompts innovation. Meanwhile, these activities are supported by traditional work practices and crude backroom administrative systems. Because system scalability and adaptability require organizational flexibility, municipal administrative systems lack these features. Even cities that boast the latest technology and equipment accept middling administrative systems and service delivery methods.

Scope of activity. What a city chooses to take on, coupled with how it defines the things it is required to take on, establishes the foundation for budgeting: the organization's scope of activity. Some cities evolved as full-service cities with police, fire, public works, and local utilities; some as limited-service cities with a smaller subset of these activities; and some as contract cities (i.e., administrative bodies that oversee contracted services—such as police, fire, and park maintenance). Some cities are quick to add new activities, while others are grounded in what has become a stable baseline of activities.

Just as the structure of city organizations and deployment of personnel would be different if they were being set up today, the scope of services and other activities would also be different. How different, and in what ways they would be different, depends upon how today's municipal officials would apply their decision-making approach to the determination of which activities to undertake. The decision-making approach itself (methods, standards, and assumptions) is shaped by how those officials view the organization and its purpose.

The end result. When these four areas are taken individually, the fixes seem obvious. Modernize the local tax structure. Reform public employee personnel systems. Redesign the organization and its work processes using new technology (my personal favorite). Actively manage the scope of municipal services. But the current approach to municipal management holds all of these areas in place. Thus, municipalities are fastened with an amorphous scope of local services—services funded via antiquated tax methodologies and using organizational structures shaped by retirement decisions of former employees. The employees who provide these services are guided by unchallenged operating traditions and supported by homegrown administrative systems. Once I grasped this, it was easy to see why municipal leaders struggle with where to begin and why the obvious fixes go nowhere.

Missions, Visions, and Decisions

Despite the uncalibrated revenues, ill-aligned staffing, and weak systems, municipal officials and managers must still run their organizations. One can gain a sense of the philosophy and operational perspective of local government by examining how these leaders articulate the organization's mission and vision.

Classically, mission statements focus on the organization's purpose in the present. Vision statements are inspirationally focused on where the organization wants to be in the future—i.e., its ideal state. These statements became popular in private industry in the 1980s and were used to establish a corporate identity and culture that could rally employees and support product branding. They also provide a foundation for strategic planning and goalsetting. Several years later, public agencies began to follow. Today, it is common for a municipality to feature mission and vision statements on its website and budget documents. Consider the following city mission and vision statements:

City of Bend (Oregon)

Mission: Providing the right public services for the [City's] way of life.
Vision: The [City] will be renowned for its innovation and vibrant quality of life.[1]

City of Walla Walla (Washington)

Mission: We provide municipal services and programs essential to a desirable community in which to live, work and play.
Vision: The [City]… the best of the best of the Northwest[2]

Viewed uncritically, these statements form positive cheers. But when I look at them, I cannot forget the mission and visioning sessions with municipal officials in which I was involved. A lack of realism and rigor marks the development of these statements. The city officials' community pride, sometimes coupled with provincialism, manifests in lofty tones and rich superlatives—e.g., "best of the best."

Meanwhile, the consensus-building nature of the process engenders ambiguity. The process facilitators, responsible for managing the discussions, have insufficient time to do justice to the final mission and vision statements. And no one wants the awkwardness of a split vote on the final version of the city's vision. So, in order to secure city council unity, everyone accepts imprecise statements that cast a wide, uncontroversial net.

No one can argue with engaging in the "right" services to support a city's "way of life." But what standard do the city officials use to determine those

[1] "Vision, Mission and Values," City of Bend, accessed June 8, 2021, from https://bendoregon.gov/government/departments/city-manager-s-office/vision-mission-and-values.

[2] "Statement of Mission, Vision & Values," City of Walla Walla, accessed June 8, 2021, from https://wallawallawa.gov/government/statement-of-mission-vision-values.

"right" services? And if some residents interpret "way of life" to mean a static, nostalgic snapshot while others view it as dynamic, unencumbered freedom to evolve, how do those city officials reconcile these divergent perspectives? The vision of being "renowned" for innovation and quality of life places recognition from outside the city above that from the local community. Such a vision may prompt the city to seek awards and publish articles about its innovations as an end in itself.

Like that of the City of Bend, the City of Walla Walla's mission statement leaves to the imagination which services and programs are right for its community. Its vision, to be "the best of the best of the Northwest," is also vague. But this vision, however bombastic, is outdone by another city's mission: To be the best city in the world.[3] (Paducah, KY).

Unfortunately, these city councils missed an opportunity to focus themselves and their organizations. Meanwhile, longer form mission and vision statements—though ultimately no less vague and ambitious—reveal more about the scope of city organizations' activities.

City of Glendale (California)

Mission: The [City] delivers exceptional customer service through precision execution and innovative leadership.

Vision: As a premier City anchored in pride of civic ownership, [the City's] success is realized through a community that is safe, prosperous, and rich in cultural offerings. This vision is accomplished with emphasis on:

Fiscal Responsibility / Balanced, Quality Housing
Exceptional Customer Service / Community Services & Facilities
Economic Vibrancy / Infrastructure and Mobility
Informed & Engaged Community / Arts & Culture
Safe & Healthy Community / Sustainability[4]

City of Ranson (West Virginia)

Mission: Our mission is to maximize services to our customers in the most cost efficient manner. We will accomplish this through teamwork, dedication to duty, high employee morale, sufficient staffing, and

---

[3] "Mission, Vision, and Organizational Values," City of Paducah, accessed May 16, 2021, from https://paducahky.gov/mission-vision-and-organizational-values.

[4] "Mission and Vision Statements," City of Glendale, CA, accessed June 8, 2021, from https://glendaleca.gov/government/transparency/city-s-mission-vision-statement.

quality training. We are committed to creating an effective municipal team focused on delivering a high level of service to our constituents.

Vision: Maintain the quality of life and the community for the citizens within the Urban Growth Boundary of the [City] by enhancing development, revitalizing "downtown [City]," recognizing and protecting the natural resources, encouraging economic growth, and providing new community facilities.[5]

Although the City of Glendale opted for a succinct mission statement, it used its vision statement to enumerate ten wide-ranging areas of emphasis. What is meant by economic vibrancy, fiscal responsibility, sustainability, etc.? No one really knows. City officials believe that keeping their language flexible will make the organization flexible and adaptable. But a vague vision statement has the opposite effect on organizations that need to organize their activities around a unified purpose.

A city organization with ten ambiguous areas of emphasis cannot integrate its activities. In such an environment, management will struggle to align the organization. And the goals will inevitably conflict. For example, building code policies, land use planning, and environmental considerations will combine to make housing less plentiful and affordable. Without an integrating framework, the internal and external conflicts and frustration will be ongoing.

In its mission, the City of Ranson expresses the spirit of an engaged city organization. "Maximize services" is the aspiration of an ambitious city. If the city organization exists to serve the residents and businesses, then the more it does, the better. Even cities that do not publicly declare an aim to maximize services favor this maxim.

But if the organization's mission is to do as much as possible, how can it control its spending? What then are the limits on the exercise of its authority? Note that the City's reference to being "cost efficient" is not a spending constraint. Rather, it is only a qualification that the (maximized) services be performed in as productive a manner as possible. Later, I will show how the quest to maximize services, coupled with other elements of the traditional municipal decision-making approach, not only generates financial instability, but *guarantees* it.

In the corporate world, ambitious vision statements are the norm, but they are also less troublesome. For example, "to inspire and nurture the human

---

[5] "City Council," Ranson, WV, accessed June 8, 2021, from https://cityofransonwv.net/227/City-Council.

spirit—one person, one cup and one neighborhood at a time" (Starbucks) and "to bring inspiration and innovation to every athlete in the world" (Nike) are ambitious organizational visions. These serve their respective organizations well because each vision is simple and unambiguous. Starbucks, using its resources, financial and human, will inspire its customers via the beverage and food offerings it provides in an atmosphere that enhances the experience. Similarly, Nike, using its resources, will create products to equip and inspire everyone who identifies as—or aspires to be—an athlete.

The role of Starbucks and Nike as prime movers of their respective visions is clear. But a city government's actions have different consequences. There are personal and economic implications for residents and businesses related to *how* the municipality obtains its resources and exercises its authority. Also, the consequence of failure is vastly different. If Starbucks or Nike is unable to fulfill its vision with respect to any given customer, the relationship will never develop. The would-be customer is no worse off than if Starbucks or Nike never existed. In contrast, residents and business owners suffer when city governments founder.

One consequence of vague municipal mission and vision statements is that they lead to fruitless city departmental pursuits. For example, aims such as "encourage economic growth" and "economic vibrancy" are common in municipal visions and their derivative goals. With only a vague sense of what these phrases mean, city managers must include some type of economic development activities in their work plans. In medium-sized cities and larger, this means eventually employing an economic development manager and perhaps establishing an economic development department.

The economic development managers champion the organization's economic vision, however blurry. These employees often orchestrate a mix of job fairs, business outreach, city branding and promotion, business grants, and commercial tax incentives. But when I worked alongside these programs, I was unable to determine how such activity amounted to anything. The economic development departments would report additions to commercial office space, local employment, and growth in retail business, etc.; but it was unclear how to interpret these metrics. There was no verifiable connection between the city's economic development activities and these local economic events. The additional retail space and new jobs benefited *someone*. But how the city contributed to these metrics and at what—or whose—expense was anybody's guess.

In the absence of clear missions—and clear goals ensuing from these missions—city officials equate *city revenue growth* and *local economic success*. Then, rather than focusing on supporting the conditions conducive to business prosperity, the city organization uses its powers and resources to encourage economic activity that generates additional funding for city operations. (The goal of maximizing city services feeds the drive to maximize city funding.) This can take the form of catering to lucrative retail and commercial businesses to the detriment of housing development or of pursuing commercial ventures in an unbroken search for new revenues. What began as city officials' general intention to support the local economy turns into a focus on city revenues and detached economic statistics.

But I would not have raised the issue of mission and vision statements if they did not also relate to the effective management of municipal finances. They do. And although an ambitious vision does not establish that the organization is out of control, it does indicate the leaders' inattentiveness to managing the organization's scope of activity.

Managing the organization's scope of activity is paramount because *activities generate costs.* Whether an activity is old, new, or newly expanded—the more activities an organization takes on and sustains, the greater its costs. Although this causal connection seems obvious, municipalities do not manage the scope of their activity as if this relationship is critical to their financial stability.

Because activities generate costs, *control over costs* requires *control over activities.* The justification for an activity—whether a new program, a newly created position, the expansion of an existing activity, or simply the continuation of an activity—is based on the organization's vision and the goals developed from that vision. In municipalities whose missions and visions are broad and ill-defined, the only restriction on the addition of activities is the availability, or assumed availability, of funds. If the aim of the organization is to *provide service*, city officials will naturally maintain and add activities in support of this objective. Thus, even without an explicit goal to maximize services, a vague vision institutionalizes scope creep (i.e., the ongoing expansion of activities) and the inevitable financial consequences.

But shouldn't a city organization provide as much service as it can to as many residents as it can, albeit with sensitivity to financial consequences? If it is unrealistic to maximize services, can a city not *optimize* in some way so the residents and business owners receive the best that the organization has to offer? Otherwise, how will those important things for which residents rely on local government get done?

Every budget season I relearned that there is no "sensitivity to financial consequences" when the limit of the organization's vision is the sky. Vague missions and visions feed a broken decision-making approach. And without a sound decision-making approach, a municipality can only optimize organizational and financial discord.

Revisiting Assumptions

Every decision-making process is based on certain assumptions. These assumptions can either support good decisions if they are correct or lead to bad decisions if they are wrong. One of the reasons intelligent and experienced staff, managers, boards, and councils make poor decisions is that they adopt wrong assumptions. Here are some of the assumptions that are made in municipal deliberations that contribute to financial missteps and limit problem-solving opportunities:

Something is better than nothing. This sentiment underlies the inclination of the city organization to take decisive action—i.e., to act in response to any issue framed as a problem. City officials demonstrate their worth by deploying the city organization. Meanwhile, city staff are eager to show that they are doing their jobs. City organizations take pride in their responsiveness to requests from community members. However, a wrong action is not necessarily neutral at worst. Such an action can be damaging.

A culturally embedded tendency to act presents a problem for an overextended city organization. The calls for the city to *do something* do not stop when it is under financial pressure. When the city tries to evaluate its scope of activity, its analysis is paralyzed by the prospect of shedding the *somethings* that some people want to preserve. Then, the city officials' only alternative is to declare a revenue problem. When *something* is better than *nothing*, it is difficult to get rid of *anything*.

If something is better than nothing, then more services are better than fewer. In such a case, an organization's aim to maximize services becomes obligatory. The operational and financial consequences of operating in this mode are apparent in cities' struggle to manage commitments and expectations. The local services provided last year are taken for granted as city officials' attention shifts to what's new. This is the orientation of city organizations shaped by the ambitious visions expressed in state of the city addresses by their mayors and the introductory remarks of new city managers as they board. Municipalities find implementing new programs to be more exciting and worthy of resources than resolving long-standing problems.

Sometimes, cities transform opportunities to do less into opportunities to do more. When the frequency of structural fires decreased, fire departments took on ambulance services. Rather than wait until there is sufficient demand to attract private investment in local projects, cities reach out to commercial firms and provide incentives to secure public–private partnerships. Even the governance structure of the city is not immune to proliferation. Not content to use representative government efficiently, city officials have made civic engagement through boards, commissions, and committees a community commodity. But all these subunits of the city council add to the organization's administrative complexity and must be supported by city staff. Meanwhile, the police department must keep up with the evolving needs of the city's residents and businesses.

City organizations do need to take certain actions. But if these organizations lack clear criteria that delimit their actions, they advance a sense of scarcity and maximize frustration.

Services provided via public agencies are superior to those delivered by the private sector because they ensure public accountability. Public input to the decision-making process and the fact that those making decisions are elected representatives who answer to residents constitute the essence of public accountability. Such *accountability* is often offered as a justification for a municipality's involvement.

For example, city officials may contend that city ownership of a recreation center is an unquestionable benefit because all residents have a say in how it is used. These city officials must answer to residents for any decisions that they make regarding the facilities, services offered, hours of operation, etc. But municipal ownership and management of such facilities does not guarantee the quality of the services or the organization's qualifications to provide a given service. Nor does it guarantee any meaningful accountability. The problem is not that city officials and employees do not take their responsibilities seriously. Some of the most dedicated residents and employees populate city recreation commissions and recreation departments. But there is more to accountability than positive engagement, a decent work ethic, and a public process. Accountability in the context of service delivery entails responsibility for *results*.

In the private sector there are several built-in factors that encourage positive results. The success of commercial organizations is limited to their ability to create value that induces willing participation. To be rewarded financially, one must deliver results. Once an organization is in operation, profit becomes an objective measure of success. Profitability also serves as an ongoing feedback structure to inform operational decisions, such as specific service offerings and hours of operation. And if a commercial organization does not deliver effectively, it will not be able to carry on indefinitely. In such a case, competition will eventually take over.

Municipal organizations have no such feedback structure. Community surveys are a thin substitute for profitability as a measure of customer satisfaction or value. And municipalities are unconcerned with competition. Even if municipalities were to overcome their vague missions and visions and establish definitive results, it is unclear who would be responsible for these results. It is also unclear how the actions leading to these results are defined, communicated, and monitored in a municipal organization. And who would enforce accountability? (Keeping in mind that if *everyone* is responsible, then *no one* is responsible.)

Just as public accountability does not work well in a commercial service context, we would not want the elements of private sector commerce (i.e., incentives, profitability, competition) driving the activity of municipal police departments. But there is a deeper issue. Accountability is not the proper standard for deciding when the local agency should intervene. We should not have municipal governments take over all local services in the name of public accountability; nor should we disband local governments in favor of the incentives that fuel private sector production. Later, I will present a clear, proper standard for deploying local government.

If the municipality provides a given service—or engages in an activity—there must be a good reason. This assumption gives credence to the status quo without regard for the historical context in which prior municipal officials made decisions. When succeeding municipal officials endorse prior decisions without evaluation, they tacitly accept the decision-making approach and values that were employed by the past decision-makers.

Does a municipality run the local transportation system because a century ago it took over transportation to protect its streetcar and railway revenue in response to the Uber of the twentieth century, the jitney? Does anyone know the reason the city chose to build a golf course—or remember the last time that facility did not need a subsidy for its ongoing operations? Did the city accept the bequeathment of a park or public art for which it neglected to calculate or even consider the ongoing cost of maintenance? Municipal officials that do not ask these questions deny themselves the opportunity to shape the future.

The majority was in support; therefore, it was the right decision. This assumption endorses the substitution of majority rule for principled decision-making. For example, in the case of local taxes, rent control, and land use measures, majority support often defines the community interest. But whether the action is endorsed by a city council plurality or the majority of the local electorate, there is no basis for blind deference to the sheer number of those who supported a given decision.

Turning to Auberon Herbert:

> Arithmetic is a very excellent thing in its place, but it can neither give nor take away rights. Because you can collect three men on one side, and only two on the other side, that can offer no reason—no shadow of a reason—why the three men should dispose of the lives and property of the two men, should settle for them what they are to do, and what they are to be.[6]

This description applies to local government powers exercised in a manner that subordinates the will of some residents to that of others. If we want a harmonious community, neither minorities nor majorities should squash the freedom and autonomy of other residents.

Restricting the city government's funding sources will force the organization to rightsize and run more efficiently. Some residents, frustrated by the extent of local taxation or the size and reach of the city organization, make this assumption. These individuals and groups often object to new taxes and increased tax rates and may even advocate for tax rollbacks.

I compare the effectiveness of this scheme to that of a starvation diet. The subject will lose weight, but not in a healthy or sustainable manner. Whether facing revenue declines due to economic circumstances or voter actions, municipal organizations confine themselves to the most politically acceptable spending reductions. Often, the result is short-term savings absent lasting financial or operational improvements.

For example, forced to reduce spending, a fire department might scale down its administrative staff and vehicle replacement funding. The city takes this action even though higher-paid firefighters must absorb the administrative chores left behind, and reducing vehicle replacement funding saves nothing in the long run. Why? Because it is politically unpopular to reduce the number of firefighters. Or the city keeps a marginally popular recreation activity because the program subsidy is small. No one wants to be the one to upset the few program participants.

In response to a reduction in funding, a city may take fiscally imprudent actions, such as spending down reserves, deferring road or building maintenance, or delaying the funding of retirement benefits. To expect a city organization to effectively *rightsize*—whatever that might mean—in response

---

[6] Auberon Herbert, *The Voluntaryist Creed* (Oxford: Oxford University Press, 1908), 68.

to diminished resources is to assume that it is ready to challenge its decision-making approach. A city poised to reevaluate its scope of activity in such a fundamental way would be an unlikely object of such a financial starvation strategy. While I am sympathetic to the frustration of those who propose such strategies, I would not expect to see a reduction of city funding sources arouse a thorough, thoughtful, and strategic response. I have been there. It does not work that way.

Faces of the Crisis

I have touched on several aspects of cities in crisis. Municipalities face unique challenges. There are some unforgiving consequences of managing an organization that operates perpetually. And there are difficult constraints associated with a disjointed relationship between municipal revenues and service commitments. These unique challenges should inspire municipal officials to be vigilant with respect to their decision-making process. Yet, the traditional decision-making approach tolerates vagueness and bad assumptions. The inferior decision-making approach brings about problems that the organization must live with for a long time. Tragically, it is also what prevents the organization from working past its confusion and identifying viable solutions.

Residents rely on municipal officials to manage the organization's financial resources. And those municipal officials continue to rely on the traditional budgeting process. Since we cannot fix that which we do not understand, I will turn to municipal budgeting next. Municipalities would not be experiencing a financial crisis without also experiencing a budgeting crisis. And they are.

3

Inside the Crisis of Municipal Budgeting

On the way to developing a framework for understanding the municipal financial crisis, I covered several manifestations of the crisis. In order to extend this understanding to the budgeting process, I will present a survey of municipal budgeting activities. I touch on the misunderstood influence of the finance director and elected officials in the budgeting process, the inability of financial reporting to influence long-term results, and the ineffectiveness of private-sector financial strategies. My aim is to clarify why, under the traditional budgeting approach, municipalities are unsuccessful in controlling the organization's financial course.

The Finance Director

> Mark, I'm so happy you are here and to know that the city's finances are in good hands.

I cannot say that I received such a compliment every day of my career. But from time to time, councilmembers and city staff expressed this sentiment. When I did hear it, I became uneasy. While finance directors have a substantial role in financial reporting, it is quite easy to overestimate their influence on the financial course of the organization.

M. Moses, *The Municipal Financial Crisis*,
https://doi.org/10.1007/978-3-030-87836-8_3

Early in my career in local government, I was surprised to discover how limited the role of a finance director is in shaping the annual budget and protecting the organization's financial resources. Today, I sense growing concern among municipal finance professionals. They see where their respective organizations are headed. They crowd into rooms at professional conferences hoping to hear actionable ideas and solutions to the challenges they see ahead, worrying and gnawing on the issues that resolve into nodding agreement. But then they return to organizations where their voices are circumscribed.

In small cities, the circumspection is evident in the division of labor between the city manager and finance director. Often the assignment of work depends upon the financial background of the city manager and whether the city council expects the city manager to lead the budgeting process. In such environments, the mix of budget participation and responsibilities may fluctuate with the organization's financial health.

In large cities, there are further restrictions. It is common for a separate budget division to operate independently from the finance director, who under these circumstances is likely to focus primarily on financial reporting and finance operations. It is not unusual to find cities in which the budget staff reports directly to an assistant city manager, bypassing the finance director entirely. I once saw this situation play out until insolvency was imminent. Even when the reporting lines are not officially drawn in the preceding ways, the finance director's role is diminished when the budget staff respond to political pressures or operate autonomously.

Often, the finance director is excluded from the team that negotiates the terms of labor contracts on behalf of the city organization. When I worked in city management, I participated in less than ten percent of the labor negotiations that transpired. This lack of participation is understandable because municipalities usually have several labor groups; thus, it is it impractical for the finance director to participate heavily in labor negotiations. However, the exclusion of the finance director is more significant than mere physical absence from the bargaining table. Financial expertise is absent as well. I recall only one municipal labor negotiation in which a calculation of affordability by the finance staff guided the negotiators throughout the entire process.

Even when the finance director is invited to contribute to labor contract negotiations, the subject of affordability is often subordinated to traditional salary-setting conventions, such as salary surveys or changes in the consumer price index. Frequently, other short-term considerations, such as municipal officials' fear of labor strife and the city negotiator's desire to consummate a new contract, outweigh long-term financial concerns. Under these circumstances, the finance director's principal responsibility is accommodating the new contractual commitments in future budgets. This is a formidable task because most municipal operational spending is personnel-related.

In contrast to what the position title suggests, finance directors are relegated to a subordinate role in developing the budget. They must *make the budget work* by finding a way to support a predetermined scope of activity with available resources. Although budget development is portrayed as the planning process by which the city's spending is decided, the reality is much different. In fact, finance directors (and many budget managers) spend much of their time calculating the cost of commitments that have already been made, such as labor contracts, operating agreements, and bond payments. This part of the process requires a tremendous amount of work that includes long hours immersed in detailed analysis. But such work should not be confused with financial planning or budget management.

When I talk with city managers about the role of finance directors and why they are not more involved in the budgeting process, I hear things like: "The finance director is an accountant and lacks the ability to look ahead." or "He is too conservative." or "She does not appreciate the operational needs of city departments." In addition, finance professionals are known for rattling off numbers quickly and imparting information in excruciating detail. A finance director's aptitude for numbers and commitment to precision contributes to professional proficiency. But such precision does not guarantee the successful communication of technical information to lay audiences. Some finance directors are uncomfortable speaking in public settings, which can make it difficult for them to be effective financial policy communicators.

Meanwhile, many municipal officials are unwilling to confront difficult issues publicly. A city council's reluctance to acknowledge and discuss financial problems is often exacerbated when one or more city councilmembers is running for election. But even when elections are not a factor, most councilmembers prefer to present the image to residents that the city's leadership is in control of the organization's finances. Sometimes, a city council simply wishes to defer public discussions until it has identified a workable solution. But any hesitation by a city council to undertake a meaningful discussion of sensitive financial issues further suppresses the participation of the finance director (and city manager) and ensures that such problems will grow.

I have been all these finance directors. Early in my career, I was the finance director reluctant to present in public. Later, I was the finance director not asked to present. I have been the finance director who inspired trust and the one who indulged in unnecessary detail. What I have never been is the finance director comfortable with the confidence of those who believed I could influence the organization's financial destiny. A finance director's knowledge and dedicated work do not constitute a fiscal safety net.

When Every Problem Is a Budget Problem

> Cities do not hire finance directors because they want to—they do so because they have to.

That is what I would tell people when they became irritated with me or my role in the organization. Sometimes it did not matter whether I was supporting or opposing their department's spending activity.

For example, in one city organization, some department managers found it easier to cope with budget denials than to accept approvals. "Lack of budget resources" was a common refrain. The public works department, having routinely drawn the funding priority short straw during each recession, showed the cumulative wear of successive cuts to its staffing and other resources. The department's standard response to any request—a new vehicle, a building rehab—was *no*. This practice became so ingrained that it endured even as the city emerged brightly from a recession. I announced that the city in fact had sufficient financial resources to allow all departments to take on more work. Yet the public works managers continued to recite the message of scarcity.

I wanted to break the public works department free from its self-imposed budgetary shackles. So I actively spread the word that the department had sufficient resources to do more and that it could continue with the purchases it had suspended during the recession. The public works director became incensed by the fact that I had effectively overridden his rejections of service requests. But he also knew that he could not argue with the finance director about money. If the finance director says there are available resources, it is difficult for anyone to claim otherwise.

In the spirit of *keep your friends close and your enemies closer*, the public works director then insisted on meeting with me regularly to discuss the funding of public works activities. After a few discussions, he clarified the reason for his reflexive denials of service requests. It was simple. The public works department had insufficient staff with which to accommodate the requests and the director was not ready to ask for more staff. The claim of budget deficiency was the department managers' means of coping with insufficient personnel resources.

This is one of many examples of municipal managers making financial excuses to avoid confronting other issues. The problem with blaming insufficient financial resources regardless of the merit of the proposal is that the merit of the proposal is never discussed. An organization that engages in this way leaves unclear what it is and what it is not committed to doing. Such an organization does not have a workable decision-making process and thus cannot apply any consistent decision-making criteria. I learned never to take at face value *anyone's* declaration of insufficient financial resources. There is always a deeper issue to be discussed. Cities cannot solve their real budgeting issues if *every* problem is a budget problem.

Governing the Modern Municipal Organization

It is difficult to underestimate the fiscal challenges faced by city councils and municipal boards. But how well equipped are these governing boards to meet such challenges?

To serve on a city council or municipal board, a voting-eligible resident need only attain sufficient votes from other voting-eligible residents who take the time to vote. In contrast, those entrusted with for-profit corporate oversight must possess relevant industry knowledge. In such private sector settings, when prior corporate board experience is not essential, it is highly desirable. I do not suggest that public office in a representative form of government be exclusive or restrictive. However, today it is significant that the governing bodies overseeing complex activities in various disciplines (e.g., police, fire, utilities, public works, parks, recreation, library, land use, etc.) require no relevant qualifications. Even under the best plausible conditions—i.e., with stable and steady operations—a lay governing board would struggle to do justice to these diverse areas over an extended period.

The private sector learned harsh lessons from its attempts to manage disparate industry disciplines decades ago. The result is that corporations abandoned multi-industry conglomerates in favor of industry specialization. This evolution was necessary for companies to manage in fast-paced environments and compete internationally. Meanwhile, city organizations preserve their multidisciplinary structure. And with recent advances into cannabis regulation, homelessness programs, and new commercial projects, municipalities have diversified even more.

The most important qualification for a city council candidate is positive name recognition. Many such candidates establish their credibility by serving on local boards, commissions, or advisory committees. Some candidates orchestrate grassroots campaigns, taking advantage of farmers markets, local events, and diligent networking. Political endorsements provide an edge whenever there is competition for an open city council seat. Not surprisingly, the public endorsements of police, fire, and other public employee unions are essential in many cities to getting elected and, once in office, staying in office. This latter point is important. Labor unions often groom their own candidates to challenge those incumbents who do not support the union's goals.

Public sector unions affect local elections and policy in several ways. Its members are influential among those most likely to vote. Union members are available to staff phone banks and distribute flyers that promote specific candidates or ballot measures (including tax measures). The unions themselves have the means to support political advocacy on a large scale. The California Policy Center, which has estimated California public-sector union revenues for several years, conservatively puts the figure at more than $800 million annually.[1] These funds influence local government policy through labor negotiations, educational campaigns, and direct political support. This advocacy model is replicated across the country.[2]

When weighing spending alternatives, the pressure to spend on municipal staffing—whether increasing pay, the number of staff, or both—overrides other considerations. Advocates for the maintenance of streets, parks, and city buildings do not reach the political stature of the labor groups. Similarly, investments in technologies and systems that would improve employee productivity are often subordinated to spending on personnel. During labor contract negotiations, this is characterized as a choice to support *people* over *things*.

Of course, organized labor is not the only interest that shapes local government policy. Municipalities are also subject to the influence of local business and corporate interests. Although these commercial constituencies make up an additional layer of political influence, they usually do not challenge or compete with the interests of the public sector labor groups. Sometimes, these business and corporate groups focus on educating the governing board on the economic impact of legislative policies. Other times, they may advocate for using a city's taxing authority for the benefit of business improvement districts and tourism boards.

---

[1] Edward Ring, "California's Government Unions Collect An Estimated $800 Million Per Year" (California Policy Center, July 13, 2018), https://californiapolicycenter.org/californias-major-government-unions-collect-over-800-million-per-year/.

[2] "Public Union Facts," accessed May 16, 2021, from https://publicunionfacts.com/.

It is unsurprising that in municipal environments populated with political influencers, municipal officials make financial decisions that stray from best practices. From the perspective of any group not responsible for the financial stability of the municipal organization, *any* available funds are fair game for immediate spending. Proposals to preserve the organization's funds often draw city council support, particularly at the beginning of the budgeting process. But I have rarely seen such proposals outlast motions to preserve staff in the face of challenges by labor groups. In the name of valuing people more than things, the things deteriorate. Residents, who are also people, become frustrated by the potholes and unkempt parks. Employees, upon whom the organization depends to deliver services, become dissatisfied with their sub-standard working environment and tools.

Although elected officials are accountable to their constituents, there are practical limits to such accountability. For example, municipal councils and boards are never obliged to diminish their roles, even if doing so is exactly what residents need them to do. A corporate board may find itself in a situation in which it has a legal responsibility to its shareholders to approve a takeover by another company, thus eliminating its members' roles. In contrast, an elected local board has no responsibility to consider a proposal to consolidate or discontinue its organization's services. Any reduction in the organization's services or authority erodes the influence and status of the elected officials. Such proposals also run afoul of the interests of union-represented employees, whose priority is maintaining, if not expanding, their presence. These factors limit municipal officials' effectiveness when the best course of action, operationally or financially, is to reduce the organization's scope of activity.

Municipalities vary dramatically in their cultures and norms. In any organization, the leadership influences success or failure by the values it embraces and upon which it acts. I am impressed by municipal officials who have enabled good financial practices and curbed the impact of narrow political interests. But even under ideal financial and political conditions, managing multi-industry activities with a lay governing board, multiple constituencies, and no means to exit gracefully from a feeble endeavor is exacting.

Elected Officials and the Budget

In my role as city finance director, I was asked to brief new councilmembers on the organization's budget. Without exception, there were two areas that upset the preconceptions of these newly elected officials. First, the spending on maintenance of city-owned property—including city buildings, parks, streets, etc.—is alarmingly small when one considers the value, age, and condition of those assets. Second, under traditional municipal budgeting, the influence that councilmembers have on city spending is meager in the short term and difficult to exert over time.

The inadequate management of municipal infrastructure is an alarming trend across the country. The threat of failing water and sewer systems, bridges, roads, pump stations, fire stations, and even emergency management centers is disconcerting. Some municipal water, wastewater, and other utility agencies perform better in this regard. Such agencies can use the advantage of their narrow focus coupled with their ability to charge fees directly tied to the cost of delivering services. For cities to do justice to their stewardship over assets, city officials must overcome the prevalent short-term view of resources. This orientation makes it difficult for city officials to fairly weigh the value of dollars directed to the maintenance of assets against those more visible dollars directed to city operations and local services. It is easier to reduce spending on such maintenance than to pursue savings in the areas of police, fire, and other high-profile community-oriented activities. This is one reason cities spend sparingly on the upkeep of city infrastructure even as it deteriorates.

When I met with the new councilmembers, I had little more than an hour to brief them on the financial issues that they would be confronting over the next several months. Invariably, these new officials wanted my assessment of the organization's financial status. I struggled to do justice to such requests. Municipalities are complex organizations. Whenever I am introduced to a new organization, I spend dozens of hours poring through documents and presentations to understand its financial condition. Even when this financial information is up-to-date and well-prepared, I need to talk with several city staff members to learn how the organization operates. Such operational information is essential to digesting the financial information. Whenever I went through this process, I was reminded how easy it is to feel accomplished when one grasps isolated elements of the organization's financial environment and how equally easy it is to lose sight of how much is really going on. I was never satisfied with my ability to communicate this perspective to a new councilmember.

Often, new councilmembers are somewhat familiar with the organization's financial reports. But there are limitations to what one can learn from these reports. Financial statements are backward looking. Meanwhile, budget reports are no better than their comprehensiveness and the quality of their assumptions.

Financial statements disclose what was spent and where it was spent, but one needs to be familiar with the operations to understand *how* it was spent. The budget detail will show that there is funding for a certain number of police officers, fire fighters, and maintenance workers; but it will not reveal (beyond their job titles) *how* these employees are used by their respective departments. Likewise, such detail will show what is being spent on building maintenance; but it will not disclose whether the amount is adequate or simply a historical figure. Most importantly, one cannot get a complete handle on what an organization has undertaken (i.e., its committed scope of activity) solely by reviewing its financial and budget reports.

The variety of funding options available to cities adds another dimension of complexity to the evaluation of a city's financial status and options. Each unique source—e.g., general fund, federal grants, state grants, special taxes, etc.—has its own complex rules and restrictions. It is common for a city to maintain a few dozen or more funds for the purpose of planning for and reporting on distinct activities. Although the general fund is the most far-reaching fund, diligent management of the city's other funds is critical to the operational and financial performance of the organization.

If not during the councilmember orientations, then certainly by the time they cast their vote on their inaugural budgets, new city councilmembers sense the need to adjust their expectations. These residents ran for their city council seats with hopes of having a positive impact on the community. However, as councilmembers, they find themselves confronting several impediments. Their bids to initiate change are met with discouraging responses: "Sorry, the labor contract requires this." "Sorry, the window has closed on our opportunity to change this contractual commitment." "Sorry, that is a federal (or state, or county) requirement." or "Yes, that idea would conserve grant monies, but that will not help the city's general fund."

City councilmembers passively watch the annual budget assume its shape in much the same way that I as a finance director spent much of my time simply accounting for prior commitments. I have presented city operating budgets of more than $75 million, in which less than one percent of the spending plan was deliberated by the city council. The remainder was considered settled. In fact, it was settled. Some city officials and finance committee members believe that they are adding value by scrutinizing individual department detail. But little comes out of this effort. Those who delve into the budget details cannot get around the fact that the organization's spending commitments have already been made.

The Budget Ritual

For many municipalities, the budget is an unpleasant and expensive ritual. Whether the operating budget is developed annually or biennially, it is one of two major financial work products that the organization produces regularly—the other being its audited financial reports.

The chief purposes fulfilled by a municipal budget are to communicate local government policy with respect to the use of financial resources, enable action in pursuit of the organization's goals through planned spending, serve as a tool for financial planning and monitoring, and provide legislative authorization of spending. The Government Finance Officers Association (GFOA) recommends that municipalities ensure that their budgets support financial sustainability for multiple years into the future.[3]

A moderately sized city can easily spend several hundred thousand dollars fulfilling the aims of its budget. City officials' desire to engage their communities has expanded the activities and costs associated with the budgeting process. Cities commonly conduct multiple public outreach events that include workshops, study sessions, and public hearings with various combinations of a finance committee, the city council, and community representation. Staff positions—and even organizational divisions—are justified solely by the city's need to develop and manage the budget. (A search on "city budget office, city budget division" yields results nationwide.)

Budget staff now have the advantage of decades of development of municipal budget policies, procedures, and software solutions. The GFOA maintains an expansive library of budgeting best practices, policy guidance, and sample policies. How can a process predicated on exercising fiscal control and supported by extensive resources prove ineffective in ensuring long-term financial viability? And why does so much of the budget seem to be beyond the city council's immediate control?

To answer these questions, let us examine the conditions under which municipal officials must make decisions integral to the budgeting process.

By early spring in most cities, budget season is in full bloom as city departments prepare for the upcoming fiscal year. Most general services—such as police, fire, public works—and the administration that supports them are provided through the deployment of city employees. Thus, it is not surprising that personnel-related costs typically account for seventy-to-eighty percent of a city's operating budget.

---

[3] "Achieving a Structurally Balanced Budget," Government Finance Officers Association, accessed May 16, 2021, from https://gfoa.org/materials/achieving-a-structurally-balanced-budget.

If the city's labor contracts extend into the upcoming fiscal year, then the cost of labor, provisions for how the workforce will be deployed, and procedures for administering workforce reductions are all known. While this is helpful from the perspective of budget accuracy, it means that most of the organization's operating expenses have already been decided.

If the city's labor contracts expire prior to the beginning of the new fiscal year, then labor negotiations will overlap with the development of the budget. In such a case, city management must propose the budget without knowing the cost of labor for the upcoming year. Likewise, city management cannot be sure whether it will successfully negotiate changes to labor contracts that provide for more cost-effective use of city staff. This uncertainty detracts from the precision of the proposed spending plan, thus limiting the city council's ability to approve the budget with confidence.

Closely related to the limitations on the use of personnel that stem from labor contracts are the constraints on the way the local services are delivered—i.e., the service delivery system. In the context of local government, the service delivery system encompasses the organizational culture, service levels, and business processes (including deployment of personnel and use of technology). Changes to culture, procedures, processes, personnel deployment, and use of technology require several months or more of committed effort throughout the organization. By the time the annual budgeting process begins (typically four-to-six months in advance of the new fiscal year), it is too late to implement such changes in the upcoming year. But once the annual budget is approved, there is little impetus to look for improvements or to suggest any other changes. Thus, the budgeting process funds and buttresses rather than prompts improvement to the status quo service delivery system.

Although cities maintain many financial funds, each with a different purpose (e.g., grant funds, utility enterprise funds, etc.), the city's general fund hosts the most difficult tradeoffs. The general fund is the principal funding source for police, fire, street maintenance, park maintenance, library, city administration, and new programs. In addition, this fund typically covers revenue shortfalls in the services supported by fees, such as planning, permitting, and recreation. Finally, the general fund is the source of funding for the replacement of the city's nonutility assets (e.g., buildings, vehicles, computer systems, and equipment). A dollar spent in any of these areas is a dollar unavailable to be spent in another area or to be saved.

When there are sufficient tax revenues to cover the city's general fund commitments, city officials often entertain proposals to add or expand services and other activities. Many cities consider any tax revenues not approved for immediate spending to be missed opportunities to provide local services. For cities that balance their budgets via property tax increases or that have supplementary special taxes, there is a loss of credibility when the city does not spend the funds that it once declared to be needed.

In difficult economic times, cities focus on maintaining existing services and activities. If there are insufficient resources to support this level of activity, the attention turns to budget cuts. But whether the organization is adding, maintaining, or reducing services, city officials must resolve the following competing requirements:

- operational funding (police, fire, park maintenance, etc.);
- funding for maintenance of infrastructure (streets, city facilities, etc.);
- funding of administrative and other functions that support operations; and
- conserving resources for the future.

For example, in considering the diverse general fund budget, city officials need to weigh the effect of spending an additional $100,000 on police protection vs. spending $100,000 on roof repair to a city building vs. spending an additional $100,000 on recreation programs vs. keeping the $100,000 in an emergency reserve fund. Under financial pressure, the focus shifts to the effect of reducing spending by $100,000 on police protection vs. foregoing a $100,000 roof repair to a city building vs. reducing spending by $100,000 on recreation programs vs. the impact of these decisions on the organization's emergency reserves.

Judging the effect of city administrative and technology-related spending is also messy. The productivity of police, fire, and public works is dependent upon well-functioning support systems. Yet, these support systems compete with one another and their respective operational needs for the same city funding resources.

Under financial pressure, there is no easy way for city officials to sort through all of the needs that compete for budget resources. They then retreat to simple, nonstrategic, across-the-board budget cuts. But this approach penalizes all departments for the organization's inability to manage its scope of activity. Uniform cuts suggest, without basis, that the current allocation of resources is appropriate. Department budgets, unless adjusted regularly and meticulously, become reflective of past decisions (just like the organization's tax structure) rather than of current analysis. Further, uniform cuts suggest that it is possible to reduce all areas of spending by a like percentage. But departments, such as that of the city clerk—which is engaged heavily in legal compliance—cannot readily shed costs. And although large departments have the potential to save the most dollars, police and fire activities are unpopular targets of funding reductions. The few proposals to scale down funding in these areas are usually linked with requests to redirect the funds to other areas.

None of these issues is at all new. Cities have operated under this scheme for decades. What is new is that limits of the traditional budget approach are being tested. Processes and techniques—and even some budget managers—that appear to do well when the organization is growing are insufficient for today's challenges. The zero-sum tradeoffs and difficulties in weighing relative priorities are manageable when the organization is deciding how much to *increase* the budgets of each department. But those same elements of the budgeting process become paralyzing when city officials are faced with what and how to roll back.

Several other elements of the budgeting process reveal the limitations of managing complex organizations with a simple resource allocation model while under financial pressure. It was during my own struggle with these issues that I began to understand what financial issues a budgeting process can and cannot fix. Let us look at three elements of the budgeting process that remain unsettled in most municipalities.

First, there is the *level of detail* at which to engage the board or council. It has always been difficult to decide the appropriate level of detail that a board or council needs to make decisions. Some municipal officials assume a broad oversight role and expect professional staff to manage particulars, while others crave detail and want to understand as much as possible. When municipal officials are not perceived as rubber stamping staff's recommendations, they face criticism for micromanaging and acting beyond their expertise. Municipal officials also get lost in minor details at the expense of attending to the significant drivers of the organization's course. For example, municipal boards and councils often spend an inordinate amount of time discussing travel and training budgets that account for a tiny fraction of spending, whereas they approve large components of the budget without review or discussion.

Although there are traditional formats for organizing budget information, municipalities have wide discretion with respect to how they conduct their public discussions. Proposed spending plans can be presented by department, by category, by fund, etc. Management can present these proposals in detailed form, summarized form, or both. The highly summarized reports convey little useful information to those unfamiliar with the detail. But when detail is provided across multiple departments and categories, it is confounding. I was never satisfied with these tradeoffs and how they affected municipal decision-making.

Second, management must take into account *audience considerations.* A municipal budget needs to be accessible and comprehensible to the public. However, to achieve this aim, the comprehensiveness and quality of the information provided to municipal officials are often diminished. A presentation designed to inform those unacquainted with the organization's activities is necessarily different from one directed to decision-makers who have more extensive context and bear direct responsibility. Municipal management must exclude pertinent information if it is to create an intelligible presentation for an audience that lacks an aptitude for numbers or who is unfamiliar with the organization's operating environment. Imagine advising the board of a technology company but not being allowed to use words invented after 1980.

Some municipalities attempt to resolve the problem of a varied audience by producing resident-friendly budget summaries—i.e., budget overviews that favor pie charts and short narratives over tables and numbers. But these do little to inform residents and nothing to give those residents an appreciation of what the city council or municipal board is up against. In good economic times and in simple organizations, uncomplicated presentations are useful. But when a city faces mounting financial pressure, a straightforward presentation is unlikely to provide the depth of information required for serious discussion.

A third challenge of the annual budgeting process is *establishing proficiency.* In industries that review financial information monthly or quarterly, the dialogue between management and the governing board flows. Management and the board can conduct strategic financial discussions regularly. In contrast, for technical and logistical reasons, municipalities only produce complete financial statements annually. Usually, these financial statements are not presented to the board or council until five or more months into the subsequent fiscal year. Imagine advising that same technology company and being unable to discuss monthly financial reports.

It is difficult to achieve proficiency with complex information that is visited only annually. Municipal financial reporting throughout the year—if performed at all—is confined to monthly or quarterly budget vs. actual performance reports. (Strictly speaking, these are not financial reports.) Such budget performance reports help municipal managers, and sometimes municipal officials, monitor projected revenues and verify that department managers are spending within their authority. But these reports contribute little to the continuity of budget and financial planning discussions and confuse those who are unfamiliar with the uneven timing of revenues and expenditures.

Finance and budget staff exacerbate these three challenges (i.e., detail, audience, and proficiency) by indulging in poor presentation habits. They often fill presentations with obscure acronyms, abbreviations, and accounting and budgeting jargon. Sometimes they present information incompletely or contradictorily. In the name of transparency, staff also present at a level of detail (sometimes with unreadable slides) that draws the observer into minutia for which there is insufficient time or rationale to interpret and integrate.

Sometimes, due to logistical factors, the budget is presented in awkward sequences that compromise the coherency and retainability of the information. For example, staff may present the capital program one week, the general operating budget two weeks later, and special funds during a subsequent week. By the time the final presentations are made, most of the city council have forgotten where they started and how the three parts of the budget relate. Even seasoned councilmembers cannot track financial information over time when it is presented in a disjointed fashion.

Another consequence of a city's financial complexity is that often only one or two city staff understand all the financial assumptions used to determine the financial resources available to the organization. When I prepared a budget, I had to quietly make decisions that affected what was considered affordable to the city. I did this not because I wanted to, but because I had to do so in order to complete the budget. Every source of revenue—e.g., miscellaneous fees, insurance recoveries, state refunds, etc.—must be estimated. Yet, there is no reasonable way the organization can review or disclose every assumption that suddenly becomes relevant to a desperate funding scheme.

In a complex organization, it is unlikely that those few who understand the budget also understand the city's operations. Many finance-oriented staff have little exposure to city operations and approach the development of a budget as a numbers exercise. The disconnect between the numbers and operating considerations devalues the budget as a management tool. And if those inside the city organization derive only limited benefit from the budget, it is unlikely that city officials and those whom they represent will find it any more useful.

City officials have different approaches to managing information that they believe is relevant to the budget. Some are overwhelmed and seek refuge in traditional budget formats; some request greater detail; and others suggest different presentation approaches. But whether their time invested in understanding the city's financial condition and options is measured in hours or days, they never attain a coherent picture of the financial landscape.

City councils then make financial decisions when exhaustion, not clarity, is reached.

The traditional budget development procedures, approval process, and presentation format presuppose a simple, stable, and secure environment—a condition that municipalities cannot claim today. None of the traditional budgeting practices accommodate circumstances that require soul searching and dramatic action. Nor is there sufficient time set aside for such work. Despite the significance of the budget, other city activities compete for a city council's time and attention. Even after taking into account my bias for the importance of the finance function, I was astonished by how little city council time was devoted to financial policy and the resolution of long-standing budgeting issues. Perhaps the sympathetic way to interpret this antipathy to undertaking financial issues through the budgeting process is that the city officials did not see value in the budgeting process but were at a loss as to how to improve it.

The Bankrupt Meaning of "Balanced Budget"

Outside city hall, one hears phrases like "City passes balanced budget," or "Mayor signs balanced budget." I have used such phrases myself. Cities refer to their balanced budgets positively, as organizational achievements. Some states have made budget balancing an issue of compliance by enacting budget-balancing requirements applicable to their municipalities. To demonstrate fiscal responsibility, many cities adopt their own balanced budget requirements by charter or policy. Meanwhile, the GFOA cautions municipalities that satisfying statutory definitions of *balanced budget* is not necessarily sufficient to maintain a sound budget over time.[4] Unfortunately, this is something that a growing number of cities—and the states who oversee them—are discovering.

Virtually every municipality in financial crisis has a long track record of passing balanced budgets. Even cities that eventually file for bankruptcy protection adopt balanced budgets right up to the time of their filing. The agencies now concerned about financial solvency continue to prepare balanced budgets. Clearly, a history of achieving balanced budgets over a sustained period is not a meaningful indicator of financial stability.

Balanced budget as used by municipalities typically has one of three definitions. Each of the three is distinguished by how broadly the organization's

[4] "Achieving a Structurally Balanced Budget," Government Finance Officers Association, accessed May 16, 2021, from https://gfoa.org/materials/achieving-a-structurally-balanced-budget.

available financial resources are characterized. For example, a fiscally cautious city with the means to do so will limit itself to the use of stable, reliable revenues to satisfy its spending commitments. In contrast, a city struggling to meet its obligations will often accept an expanded definition of available financial resources that includes one-time revenues (e.g., sale of assets or insurance reimbursements) and even the use of emergency reserves.

To take a personal analogy, this latter scenario is like setting up a household budget based on meeting personal needs through one's salary. But when expenses grow, the person makes up the difference with emergency savings and by selling family heirlooms without any consideration of the long-term trajectory they are on.

The three definitions of *balance budget* presented in order from narrow to broad:

- Balanced budget (1)—Ongoing portion of revenues is greater than or equal to planned expenditures for ongoing operations.
- Balanced budget (2)—All revenues (including one-time) are greater than or equal to planned expenditures for ongoing operations.
- Balanced budget (3)—Available resources (including all revenues and use of financial reserves) are greater than or equal to planned expenditures for ongoing operations.

The first definition is considered a government budgeting best practice and is aligned with the GFOA's recommendation that, at a minimum, "balance should be defined to ensure that a government's use of resources for operating purposes does not exceed available resources over a defined budget period" and that agencies should limit "the use of one-time revenues for ongoing expenditures."[5] The second definition relaxes this policy and blurs the ongoing, reliable revenues with one-time (i.e., non-recurring) revenues. The third definition allows for balancing the budget using one-time revenues *and* use of the city's reserves. Under such a broad definition, *any* municipality that has not reached insolvency can adopt a balanced budget.

A conscientious municipality will balance its budget by conforming to the first definition, with adequate funding for maintenance needs and financial reserves. But a significant amount of judgment is needed to properly classify revenues and account for all expenditures. For example, it is not obvious

[5] National Advisory Council on State and Local Budgeting, *Recommended Budget Practices: A Framework for Improved State and Local Government Budgeting* (Chicago: Government Finance Officers Association, 1998), 21–23, https://gfoaorg.cdn.prismic.io/gfoaorg/e4534548-fa06-47ad-9cc8-5f37e6e2f21e_RecommendedBudgetPractices.pdf.

what constitutes ongoing revenue. During and following the COVID-19 response, what many cities assumed to be dependable sales tax, hotel tax, and local income taxes turned out to be elusive. (In budget-balancing language: revenues that were treated as *ongoing* were in fact *one-time*.) Meanwhile, the expenditure budget can be misleading if, for example, the full cost of maintaining the organization's infrastructure and other assets is not fully represented. Such a disparity can occur easily if such costs are not budgeted based on what is needed, but rather on a traditional (historically based) funding level. Thus, *balanced budget*, even under the most conservative definition, is no better than the underlying budgeting assumptions.

In grim times, agencies use one-time revenues to close their budget gaps. This tactic is consistent with the standard of the second definition. When such action is insufficient to balance the budget—and expenditures cannot readily be shed—the next options are to use reserves or borrow (if there is time). In each of these cases, the budget is *balanced* under the broadest definition: i.e., resources are sufficient to cover planned expenditures.

It is important that the budget help city officials fully understand the short- and long-term impacts of city spending. Unfortunately, the structure and language of general governmental budgeting (i.e., that which covers police, fire, public works, etc.) blurs the distinction between short- and long-term impacts.

Under the standard governmental short-term planning horizon, *expenditure* is used to describe the use of funds for *any* reason. Thus, payment of operating expenses, debt repayments, and capital expenditures all have the same budget status. Yet these three uses have quite different long-term consequences. Once an operating expense such as payroll or a contractual service is incurred, the corresponding city funds are depleted. There is no future benefit. But a bond or other debt repayment will reduce financial obligations. The funds are still depleted, but the organization will pay less in the future than if it had not made the payment. A capital expenditure is more complex. It will reduce available funds like the other expenditures, but the organization will have something tangible (e.g., a vehicle, a building, equipment, etc.) that provides value beyond the current year. However, many such expenditures come with other obligations, such as the cost to maintain and the commitment to replace the asset in the future.

City officials understand the qualitative differences between different types of spending. And it is common for budget presentations to distinguish operating expenses from debt payments and capital expenditures. Multiyear budget projections, when presented, disclose the expected long-term impact. But I contrast the quality of this information with what I had to provide when

I worked in a financial institution. There, we knew very clearly when we were investing and buying assets, when we were reducing liabilities, and when we were spending on operations. It is easy to neglect the long-term impact of a decision when the consequences are not presented clearly and completely.

To appreciate how misjudging revenues and lumping distinct kinds of expenditures together can distort financial understanding, one need only look at the process of balancing a city budget. Various actions with significantly different long-term financial implications have equivalent impact on the budget. For example, increasing revenue assumptions by $100,000, deferring $100,000 of maintenance, and permanent operational cuts of $100,000 all have the same impact on balancing the current budget. However, their respective long-term impacts vary significantly. Table 3.1 is designed to capture this point.

These budget-balancing techniques are used to deliver budgets that meet the criteria of resources greater than or equal to expenditures. In the short term, they all have the same impact: i.e., they effectively close the mathematical budget gap by like amounts. Several years later, however, the impacts are quite different. A permanent elimination of an operating expense now will improve financial results in subsequent years. Assuming an inflationary factor of three percent, $10,000 saved this year will save an additional $10,300 next year and an additional $10,609 the following year. In contrast, a $10,000 deferral of maintenance will delay the spending, but not save anything. If the delayed maintenance results in the asset's impairment, the cost of repair or replacement will far exceed what was saved in the short term.

Table 3.1 Budget-balancing actions and their financial impacts

<table>
<tr><th>Budget-balancing action</th><th>Immediate impact per $1</th><th>Mid-term impact per $1 1–3 years</th><th>Long-term impact per $1 > 3 years</th></tr>
<tr><td rowspan="2">Defer maintenance; Defer funding of asset replacement</td><td>Benefit $1</td><td>$0</td><td>Cost > $1</td></tr>
<tr><td colspan="3">Deferral of infrastructure maintenance and asset replacement often results in greater long-term costs.</td></tr>
<tr><td rowspan="2">Reduce funding of reserves</td><td>Benefit $1</td><td>~ $0
Minor cost impact</td><td>Cost > $1</td></tr>
<tr><td colspan="3">Reduced funding of reserves provides short-term benefit at the expense of greater future exposure and loss of investment return on the reserves.</td></tr>
</table>

(continued)

Table 3.1 (continued)

Budget-balancing action	**Immediate impact per $1**	**Mid-term impact per $1 1–3 years**	**Long-term impact per $1 > 3 years**
Reduce funding of liabilities	Benefit $1	~ $0 Minor cost impact	Cost > $1
	Deferring funding of liabilities typically results in greater future outlays, due to interest-related costs.		
Borrow funds	Benefit $1	Cost is dependent upon payback terms	Cost > $1
	Borrowing results in greater future outlays, due to repayment of principal and interest costs.		
Increase revenue assumptions	Justifies $1 of planned spending	Cost ~ $1 if assumptions do not hold	Cost > $1 if assumptions do not hold
	Long-term impact is compounded if new revenues are expected to grow. A dollar of projected increased revenue now will require more than $1 in adjustments in the future if the revenues are not realized.		
Temporary operational cuts	Benefit $1	Benefit $0–$1 depending upon duration of cuts	$0
	No impact after end of cuts.		
Permanent operational cuts	Benefit $1	Benefit ~$1	Benefit > $1
	Permanent operational cuts have the greatest future benefit because most operating costs grow over time.		

To achieve a balanced budget, a city may opt to increase revenue projections; delay spending on maintenance and replacement of infrastructure and equipment; reduce funding for reserves; implement one-time operational cuts; or reduce discretionary funding of long-term obligations. Such budget-balancing techniques permit cities to adopt balanced budgets up to the year in which they declare fiscal emergencies.

The Separate Worlds of Budgeting and Financial Reporting

It is hardly surprising that the traditional budgeting process does little to bring about long-term financial stability. The budgeting process itself emphasizes short-term considerations. The aim of the process is to plan the spending of *currently available funds*. This fixes municipal officials' attention on the most pressing, most visible short-term issues.

Who bears responsibility for this short-term perspective? It is easy to point one's finger at the Governmental Accounting Standards Board (GASB), the organization that has been setting accounting and financial reporting standards for almost forty years. Delving into a discussion of governmental accounting sounds—and could be—tedious. However, the relationship between budgeting and financial reporting can be illuminated by a brief look at three of the nearly 100 statements (accounting pronouncements) that the GASB has issued. The first of these statements is clearly not tedious. It caused a ruckus among government finance professionals that went on for a few years, ringing in the turn of the century.

Prior to this millennium, governmental financial reporting reinforced the short-term perspective of the budgeting process. Most governmental financial statements were not required to report the value of municipally owned infrastructure. Such infrastructure includes everything from streets to city buildings to storm drains. At the time, it was natural for local governments to focus their financial reporting on short-term resources (e.g., cash) and exclude such infrastructure. Meanwhile, it would have been scandalous for a private company to fail to report the assets (major property) used in the conduct of its business. But until the financial reporting of these assets was required by the GASB, there was no impetus for cities to maintain comprehensive and current asset inventories. Many cities lost track of what they had built and acquired, how much those assets were worth, and how they should have prepared for each asset's eventual replacement.

The accounting pronouncement that gave rise to this and other significant financial reporting changes was Governmental Accounting Standards Board Statement No. 34 (GASB 34), commencing in the early 2000s. Although this history now seems arcane, GASB Chairman Tom Allen touted the new standard as "the most significant change in the history of governmental accounting."[6]

---

[6] Governmental Accounting Standards Board, "GASB Releases New Information That Will Significantly Change Financial Reporting by State and Local Governments," 1999.

The implementation of this dramatic financial reporting change drew attention to the scope and scale of municipally owned property of all types. Many, if not most, cities did not have capital asset policies to govern the acquisition and maintenance of city property. The process of preparing a complete inventory of the organization's property, fleet, equipment, and infrastructure assets enlightened both municipal officials and the managers responsible for such assets.

Several years later, the GASB issued two accounting pronouncements that together raised the financial reporting visibility of municipal obligations associated with employee retirement-related benefits: GASB 68, first implemented in 2014; and GASB 75, first implemented in 2017. These financial reporting requirements affect the vast number of municipalities that offer guaranteed (i.e., defined benefit) pension and retiree medical benefits to their employees. These pronouncements brought government reporting of employee retirement-related obligations up to a level comparable to that which the private sector was subject to more than a decade earlier. As with GASB 34, the two new statements raised awareness of the long-term financial picture.

But these GASB statements have failed to elicit the long-term perspective on city resource allocation through the budgeting process that its authors and supporters intended. Certainly, raising the visibility of municipally owned assets and local government employee retirement liabilities has had *some* positive effects. We do see the value of city infrastructure and the corresponding depreciation of these and other city assets on financial statements. But municipal infrastructure and other assets continue to deteriorate faster than they are repaired and replaced. And now we see the unfunded employee retirement obligations featured prominently in municipal financial reports. But this information does not regulate municipal budgets, even as many municipalities fall further behind in funding their employee obligations.

Why has the impact of these three accounting pronouncements been unremarkable?

One reason is that not everyone who influences municipal spending is interested in lengthening the financial planning horizon. Those individuals and groups that are interested in obtaining immediate satisfaction from current city spending are untroubled by a short-term budgeting focus. Thus, labor groups at the bargaining table and anyone with an active proposal to spend local government funds are proponents of the short-term perspective on financial resources. And when the organization's mission is to *maximize local services*, no one poses the question: How will this look on the city's financial statements?

But even municipal finance officials—those who should be the first to support comprehensive financial reporting—questioned the meaningfulness and necessity of reporting the value of municipal assets and other infrastructure. The GFOA led dozens of high-profile accounting, auditor, controller, city/county management, and other professional organizations in objecting to GASB 34 ahead of its release. At one point, the GFOA implored the GASB: "Governments cannot be asked to incur significant costs to provide information of no demonstrative value."[7] Meanwhile, the American Institute of Certified Public Accountants (AICPA) reacted to the complexities of the new reporting, stating: "The proposed dual-perspective ... tries to meet so many user needs that it fails to be effective."[8]

Not surprisingly, the reporting of pension and other guaranteed employee retirement benefits has also been contentious. Municipal officials have suggested that the new reporting of these obligations is exaggerated and misleading. Some outside observers believe the GASB did not go far enough, and that it should have taken on the implausible investment returns that public pension plans use to assert the financial viability of their respective plans. The plan administrators themselves worry that the high-profile reporting of pension liabilities reflects poorly on their performance and increases political pressure that makes their work more difficult. They and others downplay the usefulness of reporting employee retirement benefits on the municipality's balance sheet, pointing out that pertinent information was being shown in financial statement footnotes prior to GASB 68 and GASB 75.

But the recalcitrant municipal finance professionals, GFOA, and AICPA were prescient. As GASB Statement No. 34 enters its third decade and the newer GASB statements settle firmly into the financial reporting landscape, the municipal budgeting process remains focused on the short-term impact of resource allocation. This brings into question the effectiveness—although not the propriety—of any new GASB action that would remove the remaining elements of government accounting that favor a short-term perspective on a local government's financial position.

The inability of financial reporting requirements to affect asset and financial management highlights a systemic disconnect that is bewildering to those outside local government: municipal financial reporting bears little relation to the budgeting process.

---

[7] Craig Foltin, "Unrest in Government Accounting: GASB and the GFOA Square Off," *The CPA Journal*, March 2008, https://archives.cpajournal.com/printversions/cpaj/2008/308/p26.htm.

[8] Craig Foltin, "Unrest in Government Accounting: GASB and the GFOA Square Off," *The CPA Journal*, March 2008, https://archives.cpajournal.com/printversions/cpaj/2008/308/p26.htm.

Municipalities conduct serious discussions regarding growth in pension and other employee benefit-related liabilities. And they hold similarly thoughtful discussions about the deterioration of municipal infrastructure. But such discussions often take place in separate council or board study sessions. Such forums are good for educational purposes; however, the sense of urgency rarely makes its way to the budgeting process.

Some municipalities were setting aside funds for asset replacement and retiree obligations long before the GASB began to investigate these issues. Other, mostly small, agencies abstained from offering defined benefits to their employees. (Such agencies generally offer fixed employer contributions to retirement plans, thus precluding uncertainty regarding the total cost of such benefits.) Meanwhile, the financial obligations continue to grow for the many municipalities across the country that have failed to set aside *any* monies for retiree medical benefits.

Governmental financial reporting does not inspire fiscal prudence; nor does it deter imprudence. Local government is not impelled by financial reporting.

Local Government Is Not a Business

City officials are disappointed to find that conventional business strategies to combat declining revenues founder in municipal environments. Without delving into *why* local government is not a business—something I will cover later—it is helpful to examine why municipalities do not have the same options as commercial organizations do when facing a revenue downturn.

The weak link between city tax revenues and the cost of municipal services undertaken contrasts vastly with the revenue-expense structure of industries for which expenses are a measure of the cost of generating revenues. For most cities, more than eighty percent of general fund expenses are unrelated to the direct generation of revenues. The major sources of a city's general fund revenue, i.e., general tax revenues and state distributions, are not affected by the number of police officers or firefighters employed, how they are deployed, or how productive they are. Nor do revenue drops reflect a reduction in service expectations. This disconnect presents a unique challenge when tax revenues do not keep up with the cost of service commitments.

It would be unusual for a service-ambitious city organization to reduce services in reaction to falling or stalled revenues. City officials' strong desire to maintain services leads them to adopt a response of *wait and see*. Further complicating the ability to reduce costs by reducing services is that most city services are not structured in a manner that can be dialed up or down with ease.

The fundamental funding and spending differences between government and the voluntary sectors further clarify why attempts to run government *as a business* are ineffective. In commercial enterprises, where there is a strong relationship between revenues and expenditures, there are options to expand or narrow product or service lines and to adjust geographic focus. These strategies have no counterpart in city resource planning, where activities such as police patrol, fire suppression, and street maintenance cannot be changed suddenly or substantively in the course of managing available budget resources.

A commercial enterprise might respond to a financial downturn by raising capital or selling off assets. Some city organizations try to replicate these tactics by raising taxes or selling city-owned property. However, these city government actions have implications for the residents that are not comparable to those stemming from the actions of private firms. The voluntary exchange of stock or bonds on the terms of a clear trade is vastly different from the imposition of a tax. Likewise, the sale of commercial assets is driven by an analysis of the best and highest use of the company's resources from a perspective of return on investment. City government has no comparable standard to apply to the sale of assets purchased directly or indirectly with tax revenues.

Sometimes, the financial management of local government agencies is compared to that of nonprofit organizations. Like city government, a nonprofit's spending is constrained by a revenue stream that may not align with the planned spending that arises from the organization's vision. However, nonprofits can more readily adjust and scale their scope of activity in response to a revenue decline. This action could temporarily or permanently shrink their geographic reach—a possibility that is not readily available to cities. Like commercial organizations, nonprofits have the option to pursue additional, voluntary funding of their activities.

With so many financial strategies foreclosed, administering a city budget under the traditional approach is more akin to juggling than to managing.

The State of the Traditional Budgeting Process

The traditional budgeting process exposes many weaknesses in municipal management. The pervasive short-term orientation leads municipal officials to defer important expenditures (e.g., maintenance), miss opportunities to address the cost structure (e.g., service delivery model and resource deployment), and underfund important obligations (e.g., employee retirement benefits). All this works counter to financial stability. The traditional annual budget creates the illusion of control over spending—and the presence of the finance director creates the illusion of a controller who regulates that spending.

Meanwhile, the GASB can require municipalities to report all of their assets and obligations; but it cannot require those municipalities to maintain their assets or properly fund their obligations. The GFOA can recommend, and state governments can demand, *balanced budgets*; but the budget is not where the organization's financial course is set.

The fact that the traditional budgeting process has major shortcomings is uncontroversial. No one likes zero-sum tradeoffs, across-the-board cuts, or approving budgets that do not clearly relate to organizational performance and results. And no one believes that the practice of starting each new budget where the last budget left off is optimal. Such dissatisfaction has inspired some prominent attempts to replace the traditional budgeting process with new methodologies that promise more effective fiscal management. I turn to those next.

4

Conventional Budgeting Solutions

When the traditional budgeting process proves to be a frustrating and inadequate tool of fiscal management, municipalities turn to other budgeting methodologies. Some of these methodologies promise better control over spending. Others promise a more sophisticated way to link the budget to the organization's performance and operating results.

I have championed attempts to replace traditional budgeting in several municipalities. Those organizations and others like them did achieve some meaningful benefits from using alternative budgeting processes. But such organizations—with and without my presence—eventually revert to the traditional approach. I believe that these alternative processes are better than traditional budgeting in many respects. But better budgeting methodologies cannot overcome inarticulate missions, visions, and goals. Nor can they overcome the deficient decision-making approaches that give rise to and sustain those missions, visions, and goals. A municipality facing financial pressure cannot afford to be consumed by anything short of a comprehensive solution.

Since the early 2000s, two distinct approaches to replacing the traditional budgeting process have emerged: Zero-Base Budgeting and Performance Budgeting. The latter approach, which emphasizes organizational *results* and *outcomes*, gave rise to Priority-Driven Budgeting and a few variants.

M. Moses, *The Municipal Financial Crisis*,
https://doi.org/10.1007/978-3-030-87836-8_4

Zero-Base Budgeting

Zero-Base Budgeting (ZBB), sometimes called Zero-Based Budgeting, was introduced to government at the federal level by President Jimmy Carter in the late 1970s. The characteristic approach and namesake are based on a fresh, comprehensive review of spending. This is carried out by building the budget from "zero." Thus, the organization's *entire* budget requires deliberate justification. Such an approach is a radical departure from the traditional budgeting approach, in which only incremental, year-over-year changes receive significant attention.

The development of ZBB consists of three important steps: (1) identifying decision packages; (2) ranking decision packages; and (3) allocating resources. Although the process is conceptually simple, it is notorious in both the private and public sectors for requiring a considerable amount of effort to implement across an organization.

In the first step, managers across the organization assemble decision packages from smaller, related organizational activities. For example, a building code division might submit three decision packages, with each package representing a different level of service. One package might represent minimal code enforcement, another the current level of enforcement, and the third an enhanced level of enforcement activity. A public works department could do the same, offering decision packages for different levels of tree trimming or street sweeping. Departments create such packages for the entire range of the organization's activities and assign a cost to each package.

The next step is to rank the decision packages. This step can be carried out in a number of ways, but it requires that someone knowledgeable in the organization's operations and current issues participate actively in the ranking.

Finally, the finance director or budget manager uses the ranked decision packages and their respective costs to assemble a recommended budget that the city manager or general manager will propose to the city council or board.

Most municipalities do not get past the step of preparing and costing decision packages. To prepare multiple service level scenarios for each significant organizational activity requires an enormous effort. Most municipal departments struggle with the traditional annual budgeting process. To ask them to prepare the equivalent of three budgets is unrealistic.

ZBB is vulnerable to many of the same problems that haunt the traditional budgeting process. For example, by the time a municipality begins the ZBB process, it has already made substantial resource commitments. Thus, *zero* quickly becomes *zero plus* all of the contractual commitments and regulatory requirements stemming from the organization's activities. From there, it is easy to tack on politically popular activities. Before anyone has made any decisions, most of the organization's activities have been added to the budget. Meanwhile, labor contract provisions impede major staffing changes, further prompting departments to prepare their decision packages around status quo service levels.

The Government Finance Officers Association (GFOA) points out additional weaknesses of ZBB: "ZBB does not directly address whether a government *should be* [emphasis added] in the business of providing a service in the first place."[1] And "ZBB doesn't address alternative service delivery options."[2] By not addressing these areas, ZBB perpetuates the status quo—sidestepping huge opportunities to control spending for the sake of budget scraps.

ZBB is like the vacation destination that a person wants to say she has been to but does not want to exert the effort to visit. ZBB *sounds* impressive. And many municipal officials and managers would like to achieve the level of rigorous fiscal review promised by ZBB. But given the complexities of ZBB, it is not surprising that the GFOA found only one government from a survey of 413 that implemented "textbook" ZBB.[3] Although ZBB has inspired some modest improvements to traditional municipal budgeting, now is not the time for modesty.

Performance Budgeting

Following their mounting dissatisfaction with the traditional municipal budgeting process and the inability of ZBB to gain traction, municipal managers shifted the focus of budget from inputs (i.e., funds spent) to results. The budget spotlight thus moved from cost-control and cost-containment to funding *results* and *outcomes*. (I find the word "outcomes" in this context to be vague, but many in government use it interchangeably with "results.") Performance Budgeting began as a campaign to incorporate performance measurements in budget decisions. This trend culminated in Priority-Driven Budgeting (PDB)—a resource allocation methodology that

[1] Shane Kavanagh, *Zero-Base Budgeting: Modern Experiences and Current Perspectives* (Chicago: Government Finance Officers Association, 2011), 16, https://gfoa.org/materials/zero-base-budgeting.

[2] Shane Kavanagh, *Zero-Base Budgeting: Modern Experiences and Current Perspectives* (Chicago: Government Finance Officers Association, 2011), 17, https://gfoa.org/materials/zero-base-budgeting.

[3] Shane Kavanagh, *Zero-Base Budgeting: Modern Experiences and Current Perspectives* (Chicago: Government Finance Officers Association, 2011), 1, 30, https://gfoa.org/materials/zero-base-budgeting.

embraces performance measurement, emphasizes organizational results, and employs a calculated process to prioritize selected outcomes.[4]

It is difficult to overstate how attractive PDB is to municipal officials weary of traditional budgeting. PDB promises a refreshing approach that removes the municipality from the realm of line-item budgets and across-the-board cuts. Yet, PDB does not gain traction. The dropout rate and number of dead internet links to prior year PDB work products is remarkably high. Although the purpose of PDB is to replace the traditional process, the press releases touting success stories of the 2010s have outlasted most PDB implementations. Few cities sustain the PDB process over multiple budget cycles. And the cities with which I am familiar show no evidence of ever having been through a PDB process once they revert to traditional budgeting.

Why examine such a failed budgeting method?

First, a review of the PDB process is useful in exposing weaknesses in municipal decision-making that the traditional budgeting process does not. By attempting to connect the budgeting process more directly to the organization's goals, PDB provides insight into some of the problems with the manner in which municipalities establish their goals. Second, desperate municipalities are attracted to PDB (and the closely related Priority Based Budgeting and Budgeting for Outcomes). With the failure of ZBB, PDB endures as the premier alternative to traditional budgeting. It is important that municipalities considering using PDB understand that PDB's implementation problems are not simply practical problems that can be resolved by modifying the process or supplying more resources. There are fundamental flaws with the approach that earn PDB the status of a nonsolution.

Like ZBB, PDB rejects the current year (status quo) budget and service levels as the starting point. Also, like ZBB, PDB is conceptually straightforward. The GFOA explains that under PDB, "resources should be allocated according to how effectively a program or service achieves the goals and objectives that are of greatest value to the community."[5] This is accomplished through "a collaborative, evidence-based process" in which programs are ranked in accordance with how well they achieve the organization's priorities.[6]

---

[4] Shayne Kavanagh, Jon Johnson, and Chris Fabian, *Anatomy of a Priority-Driven Budget Process* (Chicago: Government Finance Officers Association, 2011), https://gfoa.org/materials/anatomy-of-a-priority-driven-budget-process.

[5] Shayne Kavanagh, Jon Johnson, and Chris Fabian, *Anatomy of a Priority-Driven Budget Process* (Chicago: Government Finance Officers Association, 2011), 1, https://gfoa.org/materials/anatomy-of-a-priority-driven-budget-process.

[6] Shayne Kavanagh, Jon Johnson, and Chris Fabian, *Anatomy of a Priority-Driven Budget Process* (Chicago: Government Finance Officers Association, 2011), 1, https://gfoa.org/materials/anatomy-of-a-priority-driven-budget-process.

The initial step in PDB is to identify available resources. The PDB process presented in *The Price of Government*, Budgeting for Outcomes, describes this step as the determination of "how much citizens are willing to spend for services."[7] This can mean how much is available under current revenue and tax conditions or how much the elected officials are willing to tax through their authority. I will come back to this later. First, it is important to understand how municipalities use PDB to decide which programs and activities are worthy of funding.

After determining available resources, PDB employs five major process steps: (1) identify clear results based on the organization's vision—e.g., safe community; (2) identify programs firmly linked to those results—e.g., police patrol; (3) determine the cost of those programs; (4) rank the programs; and (5) analyze the rankings to decide which programs to fund.

When identifying results in process step one, the municipality is not expected to have developed such a clear vision that it can readily articulate the *results* (i.e., deliverable outcomes) of highest value to the community. Results such as "safe and secure community," "sustainability," and "thriving local economy" are too broad to guide prioritization. Therefore, these results must be refined and clarified. In order to guide prioritization, municipalities identify strategies that directly support the results. For example, as strategies, "law enforcement" and "traffic safety" might clarify the result "safe and secure community."

The second process step—identifying the programs that are linked to the results—raises formidable challenges. To execute this step the organization must assign all of its activities to programs. Under PDB, there is no mechanism to fund an activity that is not assigned to a program. But city staff have little, if any, experience with describing their activities in terms of clearly defined programs. There is a steep learning curve associated with this phase alone that affects the quality of program descriptions. A moderately sized, full-service city has hundreds of programs. One city with a population of 75,000 identified 1,088 citywide programs.[8]

Once the organization has defined its programs, it moves to the third process step—assigning costs. All programs need an assigned cost in order to serve as decision units. In contrast to ZBB—in which the purpose of decision units is to justify costs—PDB isolates discrete programs or service

[7] David Osborne and Peter Hutchinson, *The Price of Government: Getting the Results We Need in an Age of Permanent Fiscal Crisis* (New York: Basic Books, 2004), 66.

[8] Jon Johnson and Chris Fabian, "Priority Based Budgeting: Presentation of 'Resource Alignment Diagnostic Tool'," Presentation at the City of Kalamazoo, Kalamazoo, MI, September 14, 2015, https://kalamazoocity.org/pbbdocuments/1301-center-for-priority-based-budgeting-rad-tool-presentation-september-14-2015-pdf/file.

packages (offers) for the purpose of deciding their relative priority. The calculation of program costs is problematic because municipal cost accounting systems lack the robustness to assign the organization's costs across a new or evolving configuration of activities. Municipalities consume considerable time and resources conducting cost studies for the purpose of setting their fees. Realistically, staff cannot perform such a complex process simultaneously with PDB. The only practical alternative is to cut corners on costing, making heavy use of estimates.

Process step four, program rating, begins with simple instructions: score programs on a scale of one–two–three–four (or an equivalent). I found this step to be overwhelming. The staff selected to assign ratings must score hundreds of programs based principally on short descriptions, such as: emergency preparedness, risk management, vehicle maintenance, compliance filing, property inspections, building security, contract compliance monitoring, bank account reconciliations, etc.

Rating, or scoring, the programs rests firmly on the organization's ability to assess the impact that each program has on the organization's most important results. Program raters rely heavily on the priorities being sufficiently well-defined to distinguish programs that support them from those that simply sound as though they do. With hundreds of programs, it is easy for programs to slip through unquestioned. For example, if a city council declares homelessness a priority, any program with "homelessness" in its description has the appearance of advancing the priority results.

Process step five, the analysis of the program rankings, is even more daunting. How does a priority three in public safety compare to a priority one in recreation or building permits? How does the ranking process deal with the priority levels assigned to programs that the raters do not understand? How does one assess a program that the city should not administer when abandoning it would hurt the residents in the short term? What does the budget office do when—due to lack of advocacy—building, facilities, and equipment maintenance programs rank low, and there will be serious consequences if such maintenance is neglected? The finance director or budget manager must pick up these pieces.

Despite all of these process steps, PDB does not truly prioritize. Rather, it sustains the organization's vague decision-making standards that allow status quo activities to escape scrutiny. For example, following the Great Recession, the president of the National Environmental Health Association (NEHA) suggested that its members advocate for broad interpretation of organizational priorities used in the budgeting process. By doing so, they could use the PDB process to show that their programs "materially contributed to the very results that their city council cared about."[9] He praised a few of his members for successfully expanding the range of what could be categorized under *public safety*: "While aspects of 'crime prevention' and 'emergency response' were certainly intrinsic to the way the city defined this particular priority, through [NEHA members'] work in priority-based budgeting, the definition was expanded to address the way the city 'protects the physical and environmental health of community' and 'promptly alerts and responds to emergencies in the community.'"[10] When other municipal managers find a similar way to link their respective programs with an organizational priority (i.e., result or outcome), nearly every program emerges as a priority. *This* is how tools intended to prioritize programs and manage expenses backfire.

PDB offers some internal benefits to municipal organizations. The process provides a forum for enhanced communication, teamwork, process improvements, and creativity that the traditional budgeting process does not. But the benefits to the financial decision-making process are less clear. If I struggled to understand, cost, and prioritize the programs, how would the process generate useful results for decision-makers? In breaking away from "budget as a math game" (i.e., the conventional focus on a mathematically balanced budget disconnected from results), PDB transforms budget development into an intractable calculus problem. The traditional budget embeds the status quo activities in a mind-numbing quantity of line items sorted by city department. PDB scatters the status quo activities throughout hundreds of programs that no one can readily assimilate even after they are summarized.

If anything will cause a retreat to traditional budgeting, it is a process that tolerates vague goals guiding ill-defined programs—programs that are tenuously tied to results, loosely costed, and dubiously prioritized. The traditional budgeting process offers all this but without the added heavy lifting.

Now let us return to the PDB starting point where the organization identifies its available resources as "how much citizens are willing to spend for services." How is this decided? *The Price of Government* illustrates the process as follows:

> When the price of government gets too high, citizens let government know: They oust incumbents, elect antitax candidates, and/or embrace antitax initiatives. When the price of government gets too low, critical public services like

[9] Keith L. Krinn, "PRESIDENT'S MESSAGE: Lemonade in the New Normal," *Journal of Environmental Health* 73, no. 7 (2011): 5, accessed May 20, 2021, from https://jstor.org/stable/26329175.

[10] Keith L. Krinn, "PRESIDENT'S MESSAGE: Lemonade in the New Normal," *Journal of Environmental Health* 73, no. 7 (2011): 5, accessed May 20, 2021, from https://jstor.org/stable/26329175.

> schools, roads, and police forces begin to fray. Allow this decline to reach a breaking point and citizens push the price of government back up, by electing representatives committed to improving services or by voting in referenda to pay more for services they care about.[11]

What does this perspective suggest about the relationship between government and residents and about the quality of government-provided services? Residents show what they are willing to spend when their financial choices are unimpeded. To define what residents are "willing to spend for services" as the level of taxation that falls just short of igniting a revolt invites the city government to continue to push this limit as standard tax policy—i.e., maximize taxes. Meanwhile, the perspective on service delivery is that the only explanation for deteriorating government services is insufficient tax funding. Thus, the municipal service delivery pendulum swings between unacceptable taxation and unacceptable service levels.

PDB creates the illusion of a marketplace for government-provided services by misappropriating concepts of the market—e.g., price, demand, offers, buying, competition, etc.[12] A market of free association and trade does not comport with the nature of local government. When price is reflective of what people *voluntarily* pay for a product or service, it is a measure of value. When price is characterized as what taxpayers tolerate, the meanings of price and value are lost.

PDB avoids the issues that we need municipal budgeting to address: the support of clear, realistic missions; regard for all effects of municipal spending; and a framework that can be used to decide the organization's scope of activity. Unfortunately, municipalities that opt for PDB only embed themselves in rather than rescue themselves from the paradigm of scarcity. But this should not be surprising. The subtitle of *The Price of Government* is "Getting the Results We Need in an Age of Permanent Fiscal Crisis." But the best result for the community would be a permanent solution to permanent fiscal crisis.

---

[11] David Osborne and Peter Hutchinson, *The Price of Government: Getting the Results We Need in an Age of Permanent Fiscal Crisis* (New York: Basic Books, 2004), 42.

[12] Shayne Kavanagh, Jon Johnson, and Chris Fabian, *Anatomy of a Priority-Driven Budget Process* (Chicago: Government Finance Officers Association, 2011), https://gfoa.org/materials/anatomy-of-a-priority-driven-budget-process.

The Dark Future of Municipal Budgeting

Several years ago, a group of academics conducted a study of performance budgeting and budgeting for results at the state level. The team's observations are consistent with what I have seen with all varieties of performance budgeting at the local level. The lack of objective standards by which to measure outcomes and the emphasis on process at the expense of outcomes stand out as two areas that government at all levels struggle to overcome. The following are highlights from the team's observations:

- Performance budgeting has not been successful at elevating outcomes above process.
- Agencies fail to link performance measures to budget outcomes.
- Governments' lack of objective standards lead them to default to a focus on process.
- The primary function of public sector budgeting is financial control, which requires a focus on inputs, creating strong pressure to revert to an input focus.
- At its worst, performance budgeting provides window-dressing support for executive priorities.[13]

Meanwhile, the disclaimer on the State of California budget website makes clear the final destination of alternative budget excursions:

> Although California has utilized concepts such as Zero-Based Budgeting, Management by Objectives, and Total Quality Management, the basic approach utilized is incremental budgeting. This approach essentially uses the current departmental level of funding as a base amount to be adjusted by change proposals. The Budget Change Proposal (BCP) has been the traditional decision document which proposes a change to the existing budget level.[14]

When municipalities are unable to successfully replace traditional budgeting with ZBB and PDB, they (like the State of California) retreat to traditional budgeting. While some municipalities' retreat to traditional

[13] Daniel Mullins, John Mikesell, Chad Smith, Marvin Ward, and Chase Bricker, "Performance Budgeting/Budgeting for Results at the State Level," Presentation, American Society for Public Administration, Washington, D.C., March 18, 2014, https://slideshare.net/JMKamensky/aspa-performance-budgeting-32014-chad-smith.

[14] "California's Budget Process," State of California, accessed May 20, 2021, from https://dof.ca.gov/budget/Budget_Process/.

budgeting is uneventful, those cities that pursued ZBB or PDB out of desperation often remain desperate. Such organizations, as well as others that have maintained traditional budgeting, easily slip into a mode of year-to-year survival. In this mode, the singular focus is on avoiding insolvency one year at a time. Year-to-year survival abandons the vision of the budget as a policy and planning tool. Budget then becomes *budget as financial survival*.

Municipal officials may express delight in surviving one more year, relishing a momentary victory. But a desperate organization is not a productive one. Municipalities that hover around insolvency risk the loss of their best staff and paralyze the best in their remaining staff. An open-ended battle to survive will eventually consume any such organization.

During my career, I saw the typical city budgeting process evolve from a seasonal activity, usually focused on a one-to-five-year time horizon, to a year-round endeavor, fixated on the latest sales tax revenues. It does not take long for an organization that operates in this mode to become concerned only with short-term financial trends.

Municipal officials struggling to maximize local services do not want the organization to cut services any more than necessary. But maintaining services means continuing to fund those services. The only way to minimize service cuts is to spend *all* expected revenues. This budgeting approach places enormous pressure on the finance director's revenue projections. For example, a moderately sized city that commits its entire $80 million in annual revenues to preserving services will have to scramble to adjust to even a small revenue shortfall. A one-quarter of one percent revenue drop manifests as a sudden $200,000 deficit requiring immediate action. Then the city manager must disrupt operations with a freeze on employee hiring, deferral of facilities maintenance, or cancelation of planned purchases.

Municipalities do not adopt the year-to-year survival approach because anyone believes that it is effective. Some cities find themselves stuck in this mode when there are leadership changes and new city officials need time to understand the organization's financial condition. The year-to-year survival approach was the pre-bankruptcy mode of most cities that filed for bankruptcy—and the mode in which they operated during their bankruptcy proceedings.

All of these attempts to escape from traditional budgeting are a cry for help—a cry not answered satisfactorily by any of the alternative methodologies. Certainly, year-to-year survival is also unsatisfying. If the budgeting process cannot ensure financial stability, municipal officials must rely on the efficacy of their financial and economic analyses to support good financial decisions. Unfortunately, as I discuss next, these measures also fail.

5

The Ritual of Financial Analysis and Its Failure

Every action a municipality takes has a potential financial impact. This gives rise to the need to perform an appropriate financial evaluation to support the decision-makers. Sometimes the evaluation is explicit, as with the formal analysis provided in an economic study. Other times, implicit assumptions guide the evaluation of how the organization's actions impact the local economy. Municipalities rely on the accuracy and completeness of such analysis and judgments in deciding when and how to deploy the organization. In order to prevent poor decisions, municipalities must have a clear understanding of the financial and economic relationships in which they are engaged.

Unfortunately, many catastrophic financial decisions survive municipal review and analysis. In addition, municipal officials often fail to appreciate the need to consider all economic effects, including those effects that are not immediately obvious. This lapse leads them to make decisions without all the relevant facts. I will examine how these analytical breakdowns manifest in major financial decisions; the municipal perspective on tax revenues; the unacknowledged cost of municipal monopolies; and the economic implications of competing with private sector services, including forays into commercial ventures. I will also discuss municipalities' inadequate approach to financial sustainability.

M. Moses, *The Municipal Financial Crisis*,
https://doi.org/10.1007/978-3-030-87836-8_5

Financial and Economic Analysis Applied

Municipalities conduct financial and economic analysis in several forms: fiscal impact analysis included in staff reports transmitted to the council or board, economic development studies, employee compensation surveys, employee benefit actuarial analysis, etc. Throughout my career, I observed that a city's aim to maximize services paves the way for the ready addition of activities (i.e., new programs and services) and their costs. But given the explicit organizational values of fiscal prudence and responsibility, I expected financial and economic analyses to constitute a check on cities' ambitious pursuits. But the opposite proved true. In fact, these financial and economic analyses reinforce the traditional decision-making process, thus enabling cities to manage their way into enduring deficits.

Of course, no one would ever say that it is financially prudent to ignore the future. Yet, municipal officials ignore the future whenever they accept financial and economic analysis that focuses selectively on the visible, short-term effects of their actions. Often, the consequence is predictable, undesirable effects that surface later. And sometimes, there are effects that we can infer but will never see happen because the organization's actions precluded them.

My acquaintances outside local government characterized the short-term orientation of municipalities as "short-sighted" and "not looking past the next election." But these assessments do not capture the consequences of applying a limited perspective to economic analysis. The economist Frédéric Bastiat did capture such consequences and expressed it this way:

> Between a good and a bad economist this constitutes the whole difference—the one takes account of the visible effect; the other takes account both of the effects which are seen, and also of those which it is necessary to foresee.[1]

Most authors of municipal financial and economic evaluations confine themselves to the visible effects and neglect that which they should foresee.

For example, when city management describes financial impacts in reports to a city council for major construction projects or large purchases (e.g., seismic retrofit and renovation of a fire station, building a new community center, additions to the vehicle fleet, etc.), the focus is on the immediate cost of construction or acquisition and not on the ongoing commitments associated with these projects. Ongoing commitments comprise the cost to operate

[1] Frédéric Bastiat, "That Which is Seen, and That Which is Not Seen," accessed June 18, 2021, from http://bastiat.org/en/twisatwins.html.

and maintain the new facilities and equipment. The standard cost of maintaining a new building or vehicle often exceeds that spent on the meager upkeep of the assets that the city is replacing. Such costs then come as a shock in later budget years.

I witnessed the paramount example of negligent financial analysis on a national scale in the steps that led to the headline-capturing public pension crisis. It was 1999. The private sector had discovered the harrowing financial risks associated with guaranteed employee retirement benefits (e.g., defined benefit pensions) during the late 1980s and throughout the 1990s. Nevertheless, municipalities across the country *enhanced* their employee pension benefits in the late 1990s and early 2000s. Few local government organizations resisted the political or competitive pressure (to the extent they competed with other municipal agencies for workers) to increase these benefits *retroactively*. Many municipal workers approaching retirement saw the value of their pension benefits suddenly surge by more than 25%. All public agencies that increased pension benefits took on added financial risk that manifests today.

When municipalities increased pension benefits, the supporting financial impact analysis was confined to the short-term, visible effects. I did not see anyone try to quantify the long-term financial risk. But this was not due to a lack of available relevant information. Insurance companies had been offering (and thus appraising) guaranteed income streams, i.e., annuities, for decades. To perform a complete financial assessment of the proposed enhancements to their employee pension benefits, municipal officials needed only compare these enhancements to the market price of similar annuities.

As a finance manager at the time, I was disappointed that public pension plans themselves reinforced municipalities' focus on the short-term effects. I was present when a representative from the California Public Employees Retirement System declared that some municipalities could increase pension benefits *without* increasing their pension funding contributions. It did not take long to discover that this representation was based on incomplete analysis that did not allow for the possibility that pension fund investment returns would underperform in the future.

Emboldened by similar bullish pension plan forecasts, municipalities throughout the country equated the purported short-term stability in pension funding contribution rates with a *zero cost* of increasing the benefit. This should have been a red flag. The proposition that there is zero cost to a prospective *and* retroactive increase in an employee benefit is a double economic denial. The assumed zero cost turned out to be a short-lived teaser rate. Soon after municipalities enhanced employee pension benefits, their pension funding rates began a two-decade climb to the unprecedented levels that we see today.

Even as municipalities confront the total cost of these financial commitments, they carry on with the defined benefit pension structure. A large part of this persistence is due to the steep cost of terminating such plans. But other factors dilute the resolve of most municipal officials to take this on. Union leaders reiterate a long-standing claim that public agencies do not compensate their employees as well as the private sector does; therefore, municipalities should provide superior benefits to their employees. However, this claim has proven less plausible over time, thus compounding the problems of poor financial information and analysis being used by decision-makers.

The results of compensation comparisons between public and private employees vary across job classifications, geography, and levels of government. Such comparisons are hampered by the complexity of public sector compensation coupled with the elusive cost of employee retirement benefits themselves. I expect that as the ultimate cost of defined benefit pensions reckon up, the purported compensation gaps will invert.

Regardless of how municipalities justify the defined benefit structure, such a benefit still constitutes an *open-ended* financial risk. Municipalities now face the no-win alternatives of reducing local services, paying off accumulated obligations in the present with funds that could have remained in the local economy (i.e., spent by residents on their respective goals and priorities), or passing on the cost of these obligations to the next generation of taxpayers and utility ratepayers.

The management of public facilities and infrastructure is another area in which municipal officials have neglected to gather and analyze information relevant to the organization's financial future. Most municipalities have deferred (i.e., delayed or postponed) some maintenance activities, whether due to a lack of funding, personnel resources, or both. To accurately estimate the cost of this deferred maintenance, the organization must prepare a comprehensive evaluation of its assets requiring upkeep (e.g., the condition of utilities; streets and sidewalks; city buildings inclusive of police and fire stations, community centers, libraries, etc.; and trees and parks). Such an evaluation is more extensive than the simple inventories used for financial reporting under GASB 34. But municipalities rarely keep such evaluations up to date. City management considers it wasteful to pay for comprehensive facility and infrastructure reports when the organization cannot afford to act on the resulting information.

As a result, few municipalities know what it would cost to bring their organization's assets into good repair. Meanwhile, city-maintained assets deteriorate. It would not be surprising to find that the cost of deferred maintenance in some cities exceeds that of the higher profile unfunded employee retirement obligations. Isolated studies that focus on specific areas of concern (e.g., street conditions) give rise to renewed attention to those areas. However, without up-to-date information on *all* assets under the control of the city organization, city officials cannot ensure that they are addressing the public facilities for which maintenance is most critical. At some point in the past, the cost of deferred maintenance was manageable. But cities have neglected the source of such costs, keeping them unseen. Meanwhile these cities buy, build, and accept (from local developers) more facilities to maintain.

When municipal officials rely on incomplete financial and economic analysis, they give residents the misimpression that all relevant financial consequences have been considered and disclosed publicly. Such neglect makes the resulting decisions suspect. I wonder about the many past decisions that have shaped municipal organizations. Informed decisions at all levels of the municipal organization—and at all times—are impossible when long-term impacts and financial risk associated with the organization's actions are unforeseen.

The Invisible Source of City Revenues

Traditionally, city revenue analysis begins with its tax distribution (whether collected directly or indirectly). These funds constitute what the city has available to spend. Cities start and stay with the visible—the tax receipts. But all local government organizations consume resources that first must be produced by residents and local businesses. Just as the public sector is not on par with the private sector with respect to legislative and enforcement powers, local government is not on par economically with the private sector, the sole source of production and economic value creation. This pertains to all government activities supported by taxes as well as those funded through mandatory fees (e.g., planning fees, building permits, etc.). A dollar conscripted or required as payment for permission to take action is a dollar diverted from the payer's personal or business priorities. It is a dollar that the payer could have saved and invested in the productive economy. It is a dollar that the payer could have spent on a good or service of personal or business value. The personal and economic impact of the loss of this dollar is unseen, but no less real.

City organizations like to see themselves as taxpayer friendly. Accordingly, when they acknowledge the appropriation of private resources through taxation, they describe the impact in low-key terms. For example, a city will portray an increase in sales tax that adds one percent to each retail transaction as one more penny on the dollar. But those pennies add up. Adding a one percent tax to the cost of a modest car easily exceeds $200. Similarly, cities characterize a supplemental property tax (e.g., a parcel tax) of $75 per month as the *cost of a daily cup of coffee*. Of course, residents then need to find other resources to pay for their coffee. Also overlooked is the impact of the tax on the resident who gave up coffee to afford something of greater personal value.

Taxation does not create economic value any more than the famous *penny-shaving scheme*, in which fractions of pennies are skimmed from customers' financial accounts until a large amount is accumulated and diverted. What city organizations look upon as added revenues, taxpayers experience as value-diminishing diversions of their earnings.

Sometimes cities look for ways to lessen the personal and economic impact of new taxes on residents by taxing nonresidents. For example, city officials often propose new (or increased) taxes aimed at businesses and tourists. City councils nationwide have replicated this approach to the point that residents pay more whenever they buy goods and services from businesses, whether locally or distantly. And although residents may never pay a hotel tax locally, they will pay a premium on their lodging whenever and wherever they travel.

Shouldn't businesses and tourists pay for the corresponding service burden they impose on the city organization? After all, they benefit from local police protection and have access to city-owned sidewalks, streets, and parks. But such a question assumes, incorrectly, that these targeted taxes fund related services. It would be unusual for a city to regularly measure the service burden imposed by businesses and tourists. When I have seen municipal officials discuss business and tourism-oriented taxes, it has not been for the purpose of funding any specific services related to these groups. Rather, city officials favor such taxes because they are easier to enact than those with a greater direct impact on local voters. Such taxes then fuel the city organization's efforts to maximize services.

So far, I have highlighted the ways in which the city imposes costs on residents. But to be fair and thorough, don't we also need to account for the benefits that residents receive from the city? Even residents who are incidental users of city services get *something*. And how about the residents who pay little or no tax and yet actively use city parks, libraries, roads, and other municipal resources? These residents surely receive more than what they pay out.

But how would one account for such a benefit? When a municipality delivers services, it cannot measure these benefits because it loses out on crucial information about people's values as conveyed by their actions. In the market of free exchange—e.g., when a person visits an amusement park or buys something from a grocery store—one knows they value what they are getting more than what they pay. But when a municipality severs the connection between user and payer, it has no way to assess who is benefitting and who is losing.

The fact that a city organization spends $100 per resident to deliver a given service does not make that service worth $100. The visible action is the $100 spent on each resident. But the $100 is simply an input, i.e., how much the city spent. No one will ever know whether a resident would have valued the service enough to pay anything for it. Or if a resident wanted the service but did not have the means to pay for it, what alternative courses of action would have been possible. In any case, the residents will never benefit from where they would have spent, saved, or invested the $100 that was taxed away.

Over the past few decades, municipalities throughout the country have steadily increased local taxes—whether personal and business income, sales, property ownership, hotel occupancy, etc. At the same time, they have created fees for services that previously had been covered by taxes (e.g., fire inspection, ambulance, etc.). Meanwhile, these organizations are paring down responsibility for maintenance that was once under their purview. Suddenly, homeowners are told that they are responsible for sidewalk maintenance, water and sewer pipes, and city-planted trees near their property lines. And developers are encouraged to include privately maintained streets in new subdivisions. Even after municipalities offload these obligations, the remaining deferred maintenance, building obsolescence, and other unfunded obligations constitute a deep financial hole.

A few decades ago, these points may have appeared petty. Some may still share this view. But such points will always seem petty when the focus is on the readily visible. The problem is not that taxes are too high. The crisis is that, under the current scheme, taxes will *always* need to be adjusted *higher*. Under the traditional municipal decision-making approach, cities *must* increase and proliferate taxes and mandatory fees. These are the city's only means to support its activities. Survival of the city organization and its ambitious mission are then pitted against the residents and business owners as more private resources are appropriated.

The Total Cost of Municipal Monopolies and Franchises

Let us now examine the financial effects of municipal fee-based activities, starting with those in which the municipality assumes the role of service provider or franchise administrator. We are so accustomed to municipal monopolies (e.g., water, sewer, emergency medical response, solid waste, local transportation, etc.) that we do not normally think about the consequences of operating this way. Nor do we consider what criteria should be used to assess whether the decision to establish or sustain a local monopoly is a good one for the residents.

When I worked for a municipal utility, we estimated that we had a 35–40% financial advantage over private firms with respect to providing a cost-effective service to ratepayers. This claim had some plausibility. Municipal utilities have access to the municipal bond market. Such access allows them to finance their facilities less expensively than the private sector is able. And municipalities do not have to pay income taxes and property taxes as do private firms. Nor do they have to distribute a profit to shareholders. But shareholder profits are fundamentally a return on the investment in the capital (i.e., buildings, infrastructure, vehicles, etc.) needed to operate. Of course, this unseen capital financing and risk acceptance is furnished by local taxpayers and utility ratepayers. Thus, the advantages arising from the municipal utility not having to return a shareholder profit come at the expense of those taxpayers and ratepayers who fund the infrastructure and assume operational risks without the benefit of a financial return.

And we should not underestimate the operational risks. Municipal utility services expose the organization to worker injury and other legal claims. We usually assume that these costs and risks are normal operating expenses; therefore, such costs are not unique to the municipal utility structure. Private sector providers of utility services incur similar costs. But with a private owner, the shareholders bear the ultimate financial risks—risks that the municipality assumes on behalf of the ratepayers.

Our utility also operated without the operational advantages of actions that we would have taken had we been seeking to generate a shareholder profit. For example, we had no incentive to pursue economies of scale by expanding our geographic reach. We were not legally barred from modifying our boundaries. However, the political and administrative costs of such changes are high, and the process of implementing such changes is slow.

There are also consequences to working in an environment in which the organization knows it cannot be challenged. But the lack of competition does not necessarily breed laziness and complacency. Although such a culture can develop, the situation is not necessarily improved when the organization is ambitious. In the case of our organization, we strove for continuous improvement. We assumed that if the organization evolved, it would thrive. The engineers were constantly involved in projects to upgrade various components of the treatment plant. Maintenance staff were steadily on the lookout for better equipment to support their efforts. Information technology staff were continually exploring new technology. But the organization's costs continued to increase. Our assumed financial advantage vanished.

The process improvement initiatives and technology implementations generated a lot of activity, but this activity lacked focus. We lacked focus. Without a bottom line, we had no standard by which to assess the economic contribution of these improvements. Without competition or threat thereof, we were unable to assess our performance. I left the organization because the problems that it needed to solve were clearly not financial.

What value did we provide the ratepayers? Unfortunately, such a question is impossible to answer. We operated in an information vacuum. Once the municipal monopoly had been established, there was no market and, therefore, no basis for market pricing. The only comparable ratepayer information was deeply embedded in the rate schedules adopted by neighboring municipalities—i.e., other monopoly utilities that operate outside a competitive market. But even as a comparison of municipal utilities, the usefulness of analyzing rate schedules is severely limited. Without a clear understanding of the status (i.e., age, capability, condition, remaining useful life, etc.) of the other municipalities' infrastructure or their operational risks and employee retirement obligations, an observer has no way to figure out the relative cost effectiveness of the agencies being compared. A survey of utility rates across municipal monopolies thus provides the appearance of *price comparison* where price cannot be established and no such comparison is meaningful.

In the absence of a market in which pricing can be freely established, municipal officials wrestle with how the rates and fees needed to support their operating costs are perceived publicly. When a municipal utility (or other monopoly enterprise) enjoys economies of scale, runs reasonably efficiently, and works under governing boards and with ratepayers who are tolerant of regular increases, it escapes negative attention. In such environments, a municipality is assured that so long as it keeps its costs from increasing faster than the local inflation rate, it can run in a steady mode and secure sufficient funding for all of its operating needs.

But municipal fee schedules are by their nature political. I have seen this unfold in varying ways. In one case, the governing board insisted upon increasing utility rates even though I presented evidence that the organization did not need *any* additional revenues. The board decided that there would be an opportunity *lost* if the organization were to pass up a chance to raise rates. The justifications for the increase were spurious and speculative. What if the organization later learns that it needs more resources? Would not raising rates now lessen the chance of steeper rate increases in the future?

When municipal officials do not contrive the need for rate increases, they may ignore a legitimate funding need. Sometimes, proposed rate increases are reasonable but nevertheless denied. Considerations of rate affordability can trump even the most desperate needs for maintenance and infrastructure funding. Residents grow weary of multiple years of regular rate hikes. City councils and municipal utility boards find themselves under pressure to hold rates down, often unrealistically, given the nature of funding a municipal utility. In such cases, it is not innovation that reduces the costs to match politically acceptable rates. Infrastructure maintenance and improvements, vehicle replacement, and regulatory compliance measures are easy to defer. However, such desperate responses plant the seeds of future system failures, emergency spending, and embarrassment.

One source of embarrassment is failing to meet regulatory requirements. It is awkward for the governing board of any local government—an organization entrusted with legal authority—when the organization itself does not follow relevant laws. Yet, municipalities do not have as good a track record in environmental compliance as their private sector counterparts.[2] Though financially healthy municipal utilities may readily comply with all relevant regulations, municipalities are hard-pressed to sustain such standards under financial duress or in the face of competing political priorities. Further, punitive fines are a less effective deterrent to municipalities than they are to private companies.[3]

The market mechanisms that support private sector efficiencies are absent when a municipality intervenes. How often do municipal utilities or transportation services strategically merge or divest? How often is the performance of their management scrutinized? How often are they subject to a hostile takeover by those who believe they can operate more efficiently? How often do they implement technologies that are disruptive to their service model but promise tremendous advantages to ratepayers?

---

[2] David M. Konisky and Manuel P. Teodoro, "When Governments Regulate Governments," *American Journal of Political Science* 60, no. 3 (2015): 559–574, https://doi.org/10.1111/ajps.12221.

[3] David M. Konisky and Manuel P. Teodoro, "When Governments Regulate Governments," *American Journal of Political Science* 60, no. 3 (2015): 559–574, https://doi.org/10.1111/ajps.12221.

Municipalities also use their monopoly powers to affect residents' behavior. But when they do so, municipal officials routinely ignore the financial and economic effects of such actions. For example, although household waste represents a small fraction of total waste, local governments have used the terms of solid waste franchise agreements to require residents to subsidize recycling. Unseen are the mounting missed opportunities—i.e., the value lost by every household that pays a premium for this service.

The need for a subsidy itself is a clear sign that the local economics are being ignored. The residents' garbage begins to have value when someone offers to take it away free of charge. When no one will accept residential scrap, it is *garbage*. No intervention by the city organization will make it more valuable. The market for recycled materials is dynamic. A given material may prove economical to recycle at one time and place but not at another. The futility of attempting to overcome the true economics is evidenced by the fact that even with city interventions and subsidies, less than ten percent of US plastic waste proved to be worth recycling even before China refused to accept US-originated plastics.[4]

The city organization does nothing positive for the community or its environment when it denies the true value or non-value of household waste and then uses its authority to waste the residents' financial resources. Rather than ignore the economics of recycling, municipalities would be more effective if they were to address any demonstrable threats directly, such as by taking measures to prevent plastic from infiltrating local waterways.

Municipalities further distance themselves from their customers and the market by adopting politically motivated policies that influence the management of utility capacity. In parts of the United States, municipal officials limit the growth of water and sewer infrastructure to control residential and commercial growth. Such actions favor the property values of existing residents at the expense of the property owners who would otherwise develop their properties or sell to potential developers. These actions also come at the expense of the economies of scale that could reduce utility costs had the municipality not stifled natural growth.

How do municipal officials justify the discontinuation of the market when they establish or maintain a monopoly service? One common rationale is to avoid a *natural monopoly*, in which a sole provider dominates a local market that is assumed to only support a single provider. Another, mutually exclusive rationale is that in the absence of a municipal monopoly, there would be

[4] "Advancing Sustainable Materials Management: 2018 Fact Sheet," US EPA, https://epa.gov/sites/production/files/2021-01/documents/2018_ff_fact_sheet_dec_2020_fnl_508.pdf.

multiple providers duplicating efforts in a geographic region (e.g., solid waste hauling).

In the former scenario, municipal officials are concerned that a lone provider will exploit its local market domination by pricing its services abusively, increase its profits by neglecting to maintain infrastructure, or shortcut environmental regulations. In the latter scenario, competition is presumed to be wasteful.

After monopolies are created out of fear of exclusive service providers and wasteful competition, residents experience the same problems that municipal officials sought to avoid. Worse, there is no longer a market free to provide solutions to the distressing results. Are municipalities that raise rates *on principle* not abusive to their captive ratepayers? Are municipalities that suppress utility rates by deferring infrastructure maintenance and shortcutting environmental compliance not exploiting the future residents and businesses who will bear the consequences of this negligence? Have municipalities not institutionalized wastefulness by preventing competition from weeding it out?

Only a municipal monopoly can forcibly exclude competition and technology-driven disruption to its service. And only a municipal monopoly can compel future users of a service to pay for the cost of delivering services in the present. Municipal utilities and other municipal enterprises (e.g., transit, parking, housing) carry growing employee retirement obligations that would have bankrupted private companies long ago. Municipalities use their legislative authority to establish perpetual monopolies that politicize pricing in a market vacuum, enable operational stagnation, and add financial obligations unimpeded.

Municipal officials also justify the organization's involvement in local services because the commercial market does not offer the subject service. That is, due to uncertain demand or other risk factors, the market has failed to attract even a single viable provider to deliver a coveted service at an acceptable price. But municipalities never evaluate how close the market is to providing a similar service prior to stepping in. And once a local government intervenes, no one will ever know when or how the market would have responded. Further, no one stops to think about how the market might respond today. If the rationale for the municipality's involvement is that there were no viable private providers for the service, shouldn't the municipal organization step aside and terminate its financial risk if and when the situation changes?

Unfortunately, once a local government establishes a service monopoly, the declaration of a market failure becomes an enduring, self-fulfilling prophecy. The market *must fail* to provide a service that has been legally precluded by a local government. Strictly speaking, it is only legislated restrictions on a market that give rise to its failure. Otherwise, markets flourish with sellers and buyers and service providers and customers.

Those who wish to see a given service provided at a given price at a given point in time may be disappointed. But that a market price does not meet the expectations of one, a few, or many does not change the fact that the market tells us what people actually value and what businesses are willing and able to undertake. When municipalities intervene and allocate resources in a contrary manner, they assume (on behalf of taxpayers and ratepayers) disproportionate risk compared to the market and interrupt access to valuable economic information.

When municipal officials suggest that the market is not providing a service that someone wants at the price they believe should be paid, such an assertion is often treated as a problem to be solved. But one should ask several questions. On what is the price expectation based? Why hasn't someone already offered to deliver the service at that cost? Is greater innovation needed? Or has someone developed such business plans, but the failure has been one of strategy and execution? These are precisely the questions that people ask and answer when their participation is unfettered. The world of entrepreneurs, venture capitalists, bankers, and philanthropists dedicate themselves to solving these challenges. But answers from these creative forces will be unheard and their solutions will not occur—not so long as their participation is legally preempted.

Imagine how differently telecommunications would have developed if it had not been run as a monopoly utility (i.e., the heavily regulated AT&T of the mid-1900s) for several decades. When government legally discourages competition, it suppresses innovation. And how aggressively would one expect a legally protected telecommunications company, whose business is organized around the landline, to commercialize cellular technology? The same arguments for sustaining the stagnant telephone monopoly utility through the 1970s are used to justify today's municipal monopolies. Likewise, the costs and consequences of municipal monopolies are real, even if some of those costs and consequences are unseen.

The Total Cost of Municipal Ventures

Municipal monopolies insulate themselves from economic scrutiny because they have preempted the normal economic concepts and metrics—e.g., price, value, profit, trade. But how about municipal ventures into other commercial activities—i.e., areas in which there is still an active market, such as recreation and entertainment facilities? In these fields it is clear how those in the market evaluate the commercial risk, based on when, how, and whether they choose to participate. Thus, it is easier to tell when the municipality takes on financial risk that no one is willing to accept voluntarily.

Sometimes the financial risk is sizable. But rather than interpret the absence or insufficiency of private investment in theaters, sports stadiums, and convention centers as a sign of elevated risk—city officials cite the lack of private investment as the *reason* for their intervention. Yet, almost no one asks why it is in the interest of taxpaying residents to assume such risk. Instead, city officials characterize the financial commitments in these ventures as *investments.*

Proponents of these projects abet them with glowing financial projections, which helps to neutralize potential objections. But one can understand how unreliable these financial and economic projections are by contrasting the approach employed by municipalities with that of businesses. When I prepared financial projections for small businesses, there was certainly a desire, even a predisposition, to develop an optimistic forecast. But the forecasting method was grounded by the fact that to be useful, it must be realistic. Investment capital dries up quickly when the organization's ability to meet projections is in question. Thus, investors, bankers, board members, and even potential employees have a regulating influence on business forecasts. These circumstances contrast with those of a public project, where moving forward does not hinge on rigorous analysis or a demonstrated ability to meet projections. Only if a bank is directly involved and assuming credit risk will anyone provide an objective assessment of financial risk.

In city financial and economic analysis, the mark of a good projection is that it supports the viability of the proposed project. This bias skews the focus of the analysis to the visible positive impacts. A theater, for example, would add an attractive amenity to draw people to the city's downtown in the evening and on weekends. A sports facility would generate business for local hotels and restaurants and boost local employment. And a convention center would carry out all the above while enhancing the city's status as a destination.

Missing is a meaningful measure of the total project impact. Such a measure would require one to acknowledge the opportunity costs—i.e., what is lost by taking the action. When analysis is limited to the readily seen, decision-makers ignore the economic activities that would occur if the money had been left in the hands of the taxpayers or used for other municipal objectives. Also, a large-scale public construction project increases local demand for materials and labor. This demand causes local businesses to pay more for their own construction materials and labor during the period of public construction.

It would be honest in these cases to simply state: A small group of politically connected members of the community are unable to raise sufficient funds for a theater voluntarily and want to use the city's resources—i.e., personnel, borrowing ability, credit rating, taxing authority—to realize their dream. Or a privately held sports team wants to transfer the risk of building a new stadium to the city whose councilmembers will be happy to oblige in return for the revel of a ribbon-cutting opportunity. Or the group of businesses that would benefit from a convention center wants others to bear the cost of financing and maintaining the facility. These are all instances of local cronyism made possible only by a city organization that maximizes its local undertakings.

The ultimate threat is not the financially disastrous results of these projects, but rather that there is no end to the projects that can be contrived. I do not mean to minimize the financially disastrous results: the $21.5 million borrowed for the Roanoke Rapids Theatre in North Carolina that the city sold eleven years later for $3.0 million,[5] the $55.7 million Pontiac Center in Michigan that sold for less than $600,000 some thirty years later,[6] and the millions of dollars absorbed annually from the operations of city convention centers across the country (most of which were built or expanded in the face of declining convention travel and which also struggle during cycles of growth).[7]

All city commercial ventures begin with lofty expectations. But it is easy to have such expectations when only focusing on the visible effects. For example, a west coast city recently purchased an empty bank building. Following the decision, a councilmember was quoted as saying, "What we've done here is have the opportunity in front of us of acquiring an asset, acquiring a building that is of central strategic importance to our downtown. But even if it wasn't, *it's still a sound financial investment because the cash flow danger downside of*

[5] Don Carrington, "Roanoke Rapids Finally Unloads Former Randy Parton Theatre," *Carolina Journal,* July 24, 2018, https://carolinajournal.com/news-article/roanoke-rapids-finally-unloads-former-randy-parton-theatre/.

[6] Associated Press, "Silverdome Sold to Canadian Company," November 23, 2009, accessed July 9, 2021, from https://espn.com/nfl/news/story?id=4683689.

[7] Stephen Malanga, "Convention Wisdom," *City Journal*, Winter 2012, https://city-journal.org/html/convention-wisdom-13456.html.

not being able to cover the cash flow for it is far less than the upside potential [emphasis added]."[8]

This statement exemplifies how municipalities accumulate financial risk. First, the councilmember ignores the source of the funds (i.e., local taxes) that made the "financial investment" possible. By doing so, he ignores the opportunity costs—whether on behalf of the taxpayers directly or with respect to other municipal uses for the funds. Further, there is no regard for the private investors whom the city crowded out by making the purchase. Then, when he suggests that any proposed venture in which there is more upside potential than downside possibility must be sound, the councilmember drops the context of where this decision fits with all of the city's other decisions that add financial risk. Over time, the effects of such decisions accumulate. At some point, the organization faces the consequences of choosing to accept such avoidable risk. For some such cities, *death by a thousand cuts* becomes *organizational and financial chaos by a thousand added activities*. Keep in mind, these city organizations are not banking the proceeds from their financial successes. They use those funds to maximize services.

When cities are not buying bank buildings, they are investigating another type of venture—*public banking*. The 2020s opened with a surge in legislation paving the way for public banks.[9] Advocates of public banks see them as a way to increase the loanable funds available to local constituencies at preferable interest rates. Some cities (and states) view the fees and interest that they pay to banks and bondholders on their own debt as wasteful. If only they could set up their own banks, these cities could provide below market rate financing to themselves for much needed infrastructure maintenance and provide discounted lending opportunities to the community.

But running a bank successfully is neither simple nor inevitable. The first catch is *capital*—i.e., the source of deposits. The Bank of North Dakota, a public bank established a century ago, has capital because all state and local government funds are required to be deposited with the bank. On paper, the Bank of North Dakota often outperforms commercial banks. It can do so by paying below-market interest on its deposits. Positive publicity goes to the seen—i.e., below-market loans to support municipal infrastructure, agricultural and energy industries, and students. But these loans are only made possible by taxpayer subsidies. If the State of North Dakota and its local jurisdictions were allowed to invest their funds with private banks or return

---

[8] City of Sausalito, "City Council Approves Purchase of Bank of America Building," News from the City of Sausalito, August 21, 2020, https://sausalito.gov/Home/Components/News/News/4866/.

[9] "Legislation & Local Groups by State," Public Banking Institute, accessed June 10, 2021, from https://publicbankinginstitute.org/legislation-local-groups-by-state/.

excess funds to taxpayers, these agencies would burden resident and business taxpayers less.

The second catch is *risk*. Banks can lend out more than their deposits on hand. This sounds attractive to a city that is eager to lend. But all lending involves credit risk—i.e., the financial risk that a loan is not repaid. This risk is real. The Los Angeles Community Development Bank, a public bank, learned this lesson in 2004. The bank failed when unrepaid loans pushed it into insolvency.[10] Consequently, taxpayers bore the monetary loss.

Proponents of public banks disparage private banks for their commissions and profits. However, profitability in banking is like profitability in other areas. Profit is the measure of the successful delivery of value to customers. It is unfair to compare the economics of private banking to a mythical structure in which abundant below-market loans are available on demand. Such a structure can never be achieved. It can only be simulated by appropriating financial resources from resident and business taxpayers. Excepting extreme circumstances of government intercession (via deposit insurance claims and bailouts), when private banks make mistakes, only their (voluntary) customers and shareholders suffer the consequences. The structure of public banks transfers such financial risk to residents and businesses. In such institutions, involuntary funding sources (taxpayers) supplant voluntary bondholders and lenders.

Proponents of public banking have an explicit goal that "[b]anking and credit become public utilities."[11] Further, they assert that "[a] government that owns its own bank can keep the interest and reinvest it locally, resulting in potential public savings of 35–40%."[12] If that savings estimate sounds familiar, it is. Apparently, my former utility employer is not the only organization that believes that public agencies have a 35–40% financial advantage over the private sector. But when all effects are counted, this "advantage" quickly disappears. All that remains are the transfers of wealth from and transfers of credit risk to residents.

Again, under the traditional missions, visions, and decision-making approach, there is no end to proposals for such ventures. And there is no end to the inadequate financial and economic analysis used to justify them.

---

[10] Robert Krol and Shirley Svorney, "The Collapse of a Noble Idea," *Regulation*, Winter 2004–2005, 30, https://cato.org/sites/cato.org/files/serials/files/regulation/2004/12/v27n4-3.pdf.

[11] Ellen Brown, quoted in "Two Banking Models – Public and Private," Public Banking Institute, accessed June 10, 2021, from https://publicbankinginstitute.org/intro-to-public-banking/.

[12] Ellen Brown, quoted in "Two Banking Models—Public and Private," Public Banking Institute, accessed June 10, 2021, from https://publicbankinginstitute.org/intro-to-public-banking/.

Analyzing Other Services and Activities

As municipalities advance their local services, municipal officials neglect the organization's impact on private sector services. For example, a city may institute a childcare program in response to available grant funding. Once it does so, there is a smaller consumer market to attract for-profit and nonprofit childcare providers. This impact is not part of the city's analysis. Even without instituting a monopoly, the city organization hinders the market in this way. The presence of the city organization in recreation and senior programs similarly discourages nonprofit organizations from developing and offering their best services.

Is there a significant difference between childcare and recreation services provided through the city organization as against a local nonprofit or for-profit firm? After all, they draw from the same pool of employees. And, in the cities I have worked, most residents hold these services in high regard no matter who provides them. But a complete picture includes *all* the effects of the city organization's involvement in these activities.

The structure of a city organization is designed around its primary government role and not around the efficient delivery of local services. State law prescribes the way the organization operates, based on its governmental status. Examples of special requirements include public records management; election administration; public meeting protocol; civil service and civil service-like workforce hiring and management rules; general law and city charter provisions (including jurisdictional definitions); etc. While there may be questionable but modifiable requirements embedded in some of these areas (e.g., antiquated charter provisions), a government organization must maintain a structure that is appropriate for a public agency with local powers and authority.

Naturally, the municipal employee culture emphasizes deference to the organization's governing rules and processes. This orientation is proper, but it is incompatible with the flexibility and focus required for efficient service delivery. Government purchasing, contracting, and hiring processes are notoriously slow in comparison to those of the private sector. A government cannot strategically merge with or purchase a company that would provide it with an advantage in service delivery. Nor can it readily modify its geographic reach. These factors have an impact on cost-effective service delivery, particularly over the long term. But no one should be taken aback. The structure and aims of local government are different from those of the private sector.

Government operates as a bureaucracy with ample red tape for good reason. The freedom of residents would be threatened if the local legislative and enforcement authority operated in an entrepreneurial, experimental, covert, or flexible manner. When the city undertakes services and other activities, it should not be surprising that the organization values process and rule-following over efficiency and the nonexistent bottom line. In contrast, a private organization that controls its design, management, and governance can readily adapt to technology, markets, and customer needs. In the absence of a strategic benefit, such private organizations do not have to manage across multiple service areas. Thus, nonprofit and for-profit firms can administer their services and other activities more efficiently and effectively than public agencies not because they are *better*, but because they are *different*.

The service delivery challenges faced by municipal organizations are clear when one looks at any organizational cost study used to set fees. Operating departments (e.g., police, fire, public works, recreation, building, planning, etc.) bear the overhead costs of the city council, city manager, city attorney, and city clerk as well as the support costs of the finance, human resources, and technology functions. In contrast, private sector managers have the advantage of designing their organizations around the industry in which they operate; thus, they avoid unnecessary costs and complexities. Further, a private firm can make rapid organizational adjustments in response to changing demand, competition, and technology.

The cities with which I am acquainted estimate that their recreation departments are two-thirds supported by program fees, with local taxes making up the difference. The actual ratio of fees to tax support hovers lower than these estimates because subsidy calculations rarely include the full costs. Omitted costs become clear when the city must renovate or replace the facilities upon which fee revenues depend as buildings and sports venues reach the end of their useful lives. Also missing from these calculations are the unfunded retirement benefits earned by those city employees who support these programs. Even if the city were to end all recreation programs, these obligations would persist.

City residents continue to subsidize recreation programs. But the subsidies are not needed to make up for an inability of private individuals or groups to deliver such services. The subsidies are needed to offset the premium cost of providing services through a municipal organization. The city will require future tax subsidies to pay for deferred maintenance and accumulated employee retirement obligations. Meanwhile, program participants do not benefit from the full value of what the nonprofit and for-profit worlds can create across city boundaries. Although it is common for cities to offer recreation programs to nonresidents, the fact that each city organizes within its jurisdiction hinders economies of scale.

There are additional, unseen effects. For example, the dollars not available to the residents whose children do not take part in the city's sports offerings. And the dollars not available to the residents whose children take part in the sport but do so at a competitive level that is incompatible with that of the city programs. Just because no one will see what would have happened with those dollars does not make the impact on the residents less real.

Library and senior services are hampered by the same economic impacts of providing services via the city organization. A sizable part of the funding of these services is lost to the cost of operating within the legal framework of the city organization. Also, like other city services, these areas tend to focus on observable outputs: open library hours, number of books checked out, number of meals served to seniors, number of programs and events, etc. But when city management makes outputs the measure of success, it is easy for user satisfaction to become a secondary concern. In contrast, private businesses and nonprofits, by their nature, cannot afford to neglect the customers and supporters upon whom they depend.

We have imposed a disservice upon residents by constraining the benefits of recreation, childcare, library, and senior services by the capacity and creative limitations of the city organization. When my wife and I were raising children, it was important to have a variety of recreational options nearby. And yes, we wanted to live in a community in which those who cannot afford to buy books would have access to them. And yes, we wanted to live in a city in which there would be support to the senior community—a consideration that becomes more important each year. We also wanted to live in a city in which we would have access to food stores, gas stations, home supplies, and restaurants. City organizations do not declare market or nonprofit failures in these important categories—and such areas thrive.

Anything can be framed as a market failure, particularly by a city organization with a proclivity to maximize the local services that it oversees. The market has failed to offer low-cost transportation to residents who want to travel from A to B. The market has failed to offer low-cost bridge classes. The market has failed to offer after-school daycare. The market has failed to offer activities for seniors. Nonprofit organizations have failed to offer free computer and internet access during the day. This perspective has dominated municipal decision-making to the point that now no one asks why the community would not find a way to fulfill the values most important to residents. But each declaration of market failure comes at a steep price: the unseen costs of foreclosed market solutions—costs that continue to grow.

By disregarding the unseen costs and casualties, the deck is stacked firmly against good judgment. Under such conditions, financial and economic analysis cannot help. Nor can the market compete with a fanciful vision of a local service that is evaluated without regard for *all* of its effects on residents. In the face of such reverie, anyone's attempts to point out the unseen appear to be gratuitously negative and narrow. When only the readily seen and projected benefits of city services are considered, a city council decision to provide or expand a service appears benevolent or, at worst, innocuous.

A company knows it is time to cease offering a product or service when it can no longer compete effectively. Obsolescence is an ongoing threat. A nonprofit that has fulfilled its mission has no reason to continue running, while one whose donors have dried up has no means to continue. In contrast, a city insulates itself from such regulating dynamics.

Sometimes, the problem with municipal decision-making is not poor financial analysis but, rather, *no* financial analysis. In such cases, the municipality develops a plan of action without analyzing its options. For example, when city facilities become obsolete, the common, reflexive response is to build new ones. City officials then consider various construction alternatives and their respective costs. But this approach embraces a bias toward fixed physical centers and municipal facility ownership. I cringe when I see cities constructing new facilities without a thorough examination of the options. Building fire stations in the twenty-first century to house staff is grossly inefficient. Firefighter shifts of ten or twelve hours, rather than twenty-four, would simplify building requirements. By examining site requirements, city management could also identify options for moveable stations that are responsive to the growth of the city and other factors that affect emergency response times.

Even in situations in which there is a persuasive case for a fixed facility location, the poor record that cities have in maintaining their own buildings—and in the planning for eventual replacement—should motivate city officials to abandon the borrow-design-build-neglect-repeat model of managing municipal facilities. The traditional focus of new city facility projects is on the visible and culminates in groundbreaking and ribbon-cutting celebrations. These projects are easy to justify financially because they only compete with themselves. Unseen are the opportunities missed when city officials defer to the traditions that allow such projects to proceed unchallenged. For decision-makers to challenge such traditions would be groundbreaking and utterly worth celebrating.

Defining Financial Sustainability

The municipal decisions that led to the mounting obligations, unsuccessful commercial ventures, and overextended local service commitments all survived the organizations' financial and economic analyses. In the past, municipalities expressed their commitment to fiscal discipline by calling out their conservative approach to taking on financial commitments and their dedication to prudent spending. Today, municipal officials employ the ominous term: *financial sustainability*. This term is commonly used in descriptions of city council goals and in public budget discussions. Meanwhile, many cities have prepared financial (or fiscal) sustainability plans to support the budgeting process.

Yet, no one explains what they mean by *financial sustainability*. What exactly is the city attempting to sustain? How would one measure success? What is the best way to frame the city organization's financial stability from the perspective of residents and businesses? In the absence of a working definition, it is unclear how a city organization should implement and manage a financial sustainability plan—or whether such a plan is even a suitable pursuit as conceived.

Although the Government Finance Officers Association (GFOA) does not provide a formal definition, it does recommend that "each government should define 'sustainability' for itself" and offers that "[a] starting point for the definition of financial sustainability is a government's ability to manage its finances so it can meet its spending commitments, both now and in the future, and whether it ensures future generations of taxpayers do not face an unmanageable bill for government services provided to the current generation."[13] I am troubled by the moral implications of bequeathing financial burden to future generations, so long as it is not "unmanageable" (an ambiguous term). However, I share the desire to see local governments define the terms that make their way into organizational goals, policies, and financial action plans.

Despite the GFOA's guidance, municipalities have failed to define *financial sustainability*. The common feature that I see in cities' approaches to financial sustainability is the aim to preserve the status quo—i.e., the organization, its services and activities, and its service-delivery model. When cities project their future spending, they treat *spending commitments* broadly. Bond payments due in five years are clearly spending commitments. But under the

[13] "Role of the Finance Officer in Supporting Fiscal Sustainability," Government Finance Officers Association, accessed May 18, 2021, from https://gfoa.org/materials/role-of-the-finance-officer-in-supporting-fiscal-sustainability.

prevalent municipal approach, so is funding the current array of services in its current form. Thus, cities equate *financial sustainability* with the preservation of the city organization, its activities, and its practices as they are.

But consider the implications of preserving the city organization *as it is*. Preserving the status quo cannot actually involve freezing city activities. The issues and activities in which the city engages are too dynamic to make such a proposition possible. It can only mean preserving the aim of *maximizing city services*. The result is the reinforcement of a flawed decision-making approach that fastens a city in its current mode—a mode that can only be supported by additional taxes and fees. Consequently, some variation of *increase revenues* appears prominently in every municipal financial sustainability plan.

Meanwhile, city officials gain little by strategizing over the long-term financial stability of the city organization—or even wrestling with the definition of financial sustainability—so long as the city's mission is unfounded and open-ended.

Foreseeable Future

Is it not the precise role of a city organization to fill in the gaps in services that the commercial markets and nonprofits do not fulfill, yet are needed by the community? Can't we learn from recent mistakes, retool, and better orchestrate the best of all worlds—i.e., finding the right mix of what local government, private businesses, and nonprofits have to offer? Notwithstanding past missteps, isn't there a good reason to continue these services in some form? Aren't we forgetting why the local government chose to take on these activities in the first place?

Or do all of these questions emerge from the same decision-making approach that led municipalities to their current brink?

The ritual of superficial financial analysis does not improve financial decisions. Municipalities will improve their future when they stop ignoring it. Municipal officials need to respect the future by incorporating what they should foresee and by considering all facts and all impacts. And this includes the fact that when a municipality intervenes in a market, it makes market analysis impossible. Only then will municipalities improve the quality and usefulness of their financial and economic analyses.

Next, I will examine the financial remedies that municipalities undertake in the wake of failed budgeting methodologies and inadequate financial decision support.

6

Bankrupt Financial Remedies

With redesigned budgeting processes and financial and economic analysis failing to support municipalities' long-term financial stability, municipal officials look elsewhere. This is a welcome relief to those involved. Whether due to a numbers phobia, frustration with zero-sum alternatives, or fatigue from dry, detailed process steps—most people inside and outside the municipal organization are uneasy with *any* budgeting process. And such people are likewise unfulfilled by the quality of financial and economic analysis. So municipalities turn to alternative financial remedies: operational improvements; privatization; community engagement; data access and transparency; financial health evaluations; and other approaches to achieving financial stability.

As with the alternative budgeting methodologies, the failing of these conventional remedies is not that they do not take on genuine issues. Financial accountability, operational effectiveness, transparency in government, and a better method for managing municipal resources are all legitimate aims. Thus, we should not be surprised when these remedies yield some degree of success. But not every action that moves the needle positively in these areas is productive in a crisis. When municipal officials implement these remedies, they become satisfied that they have addressed the organization's financial turmoil. So satisfied, that they refrain from digging deeper at a time when deeper digging is needed desperately.

The common element holding back conventional solutions is that they address *how the organization does things* without making reference to *why*

M. Moses, *The Municipal Financial Crisis*,
https://doi.org/10.1007/978-3-030-87836-8_6

it does those things. If municipal officials remain stuck in managing *how* the work is done, what appears to be progress is only baby steps in the approximate direction of vague organizational goals.

I have taken part in the implementation of the common financial remedies that—as with the budgeting process alternatives—I characterize as *nonsolutions*. Some, like those promising better use of technology and improved service delivery, are compelling to me. But even when these initiatives are successful on their own terms, I realized that they were insufficient to influence the long-term financial course of the organization. Today, municipal officials cannot afford to misjudge the efficacy of any proposed financial solution. It is vital that all local government stakeholders be able to distinguish a solution from a nonsolution.

Let us look at the financial remedies that municipalities rely on to improve their financial condition.

Operational Improvements (Technology and Process Efficiencies)

Of all the *nonsolutions*, the pursuit of operational improvements has always fascinated me. Perhaps my undergraduate studies in industrial engineering nurtured a process design and improvement orientation. Maybe it is because my professional responsibilities usually involved overseeing operational areas with legacy systems and procedures in need of updating. In my early career, I aided small businesses with the automation of their accounting systems as computers supplanted bookkeepers and provided better tools for management reporting and financial analysis. But when I transitioned to municipal government, I was struck by how the use of technology and the science of work process design trailed the rest of the world by many years.

The design of local government technology systems reflects municipalities' prevailing piecemeal approach to the accumulation of software. It is common for municipal computer systems to consist of a patchwork of overlapping systems (e.g., work order, customer relationship management, transaction processing, etc.) that are geared to each department's preferences but that do not readily coordinate or integrate. One consequence of this fragmentation is that an outside user of city services is a *customer* of each city department and not of the organization. At some point, the labyrinth of systems becomes difficult to inventory, much less streamline and support. Private companies that operate this way eventually find their focus and settle down—or they sell or fold. Municipal information technology departments persevere.

As a manager, I learned that senseless procedures and inadequate systems convey a message to the organization that the leadership does not value staff productivity. I also learned that a commitment to providing employees with proper and reliable tools to support their work boosts both productivity and morale. The productivity bottleneck is not due to the inability or unwillingness of staff to identify potential improvements. They know what keeps them from being more productive. I can enter any municipal organization and, after asking a few open-ended questions during interviews with a sampling of staff, walk away with a lengthy list of opportunities to improve the efficiencies of work processes. Except for a few employees whose capacity to embrace new challenges had atrophied—aided by managers who enabled their stagnation—I did not find staff resistance to change to be a serious deterrent to operational improvements.

As with financial sustainability, the lack of success in achieving operational efficiencies is not because municipalities refuse to recognize its importance. References to operational efficiency (and effectiveness) populate most municipal mission or vision statements. But even when municipalities conduct process mapping and continuous improvement initiatives, pursue better data management and dynamic reporting, establish social media presence enhanced with digital citizen apps, etc.—the benefits are elusive.

So, if municipalities acknowledge the importance of operational improvements, their employees are willing to change, and so much is at stake—why are these organizations a decade or more behind in the use of technology and modern work processes? Why do organizations that expect to be around perpetually not organize around integrated systems and continuous improvement?

It took me several years to understand the simple, unstated protocol: In the absence of a clear political directive, the burden is on the one who proposes to disturb the status quo. My antipathy to underperforming work processes was an incomprehensible motivation in an organizational culture adapted to political perception. In a culture moved by the political, everyone is assumed to have a political motive. Rather than valued as progress, initiatives requiring change are met with suspicion. "If this proposed change is such a promising idea," one councilmember wondered aloud, "why haven't we already implemented it?"

The reason municipalities do not implement promising ideas is that they treat new ideas as threats before considering them to be opportunities. The only *real* opportunities are *political* opportunities. This bias is not sufficient to preempt every good operational idea. Some good operational ideas are politically popular. But any leaning that hinders operational improvements stunts the organization. The organization is mired in a conflict: its leaders say that they want a modern, efficient organization, but they favor the traditional way of operating. Meanwhile, the low threshold for taking on more activities (i.e., maximize local services) overwhelms the intransigent organization.

Municipalities are not poised to benefit financially when they successfully implement new technology and streamline operations. The elimination of, or modification to, a work process that saves one thousand hours of staff time per year is unlikely to result in reduced personnel costs. City staffing schemes are not designed to capture such savings. Though no one ever proves it, time freed up from improved processes and technology is assumed to shift to higher level work. Such an assumption would be more credible if the workforce were more flexible. Thus, even successful time saving improvements do not advance the organization in a meaningful way.

It is tempting to plunge into operational streamlining and technology solutions and assume that the organization's mission and scope of activity are appropriate. I found myself having to do this simply to keep operational processes from stagnating. But this approach reinforces the status quo—the same status quo mission and scope of activity that *is* the crisis to be addressed. Improving service delivery through better processes and use of technology will only be of value to residents and businesses if the processes being improved support a proper organizational scope of activity.

Service Delivery Restructuring: Privatization and Regionalization

Beyond improvements to technology and work processes, municipalities often make structural changes to the way services are delivered. Such changes sometimes take the form of *privatization*—which encompasses asset sales and transfer agreements as well as outsourcing contracts for operations, maintenance, and other activities. A change in service delivery can also take the form of *regionalization*—the temporary or permanent consolidation or sharing of municipal services and administration.

Privatization

Privatization can refer to a permanent or temporary transfer of services or assets from government to the private sector, a complete or partial transfer of services or assets from government to the private sector, or the contractual outsourcing of internal support functions. Thus, privatization includes a city government's wholesale withdrawal from an activity (e.g., transportation, recreation, childcare services), the sale of public facilities (e.g., golf course, surplus property), long-term operating and maintenance contracts (e.g., water, wastewater, electric, solid waste and recycling), and service contracts (e.g., building inspection, planning, meter installation and reading, building maintenance, fleet management, recruitment, payroll services, etc.).

The following advice from *Reinventing Government* three decades ago renewed discussions regarding the sale of city assets, the formation of long-term operations agreements, and a broad range of outsourcing activities:

> It makes sense to put the delivery of many public services in private hands (whether for-profit or nonprofit), if by doing so a government can get more effectiveness, efficiency, equity or accountability.[1]

Whenever someone puts forth privatization as a solution, a polarizing debate often ensues. (The fact that privatization can refer to a broad range of transactions and arrangements only complicates the discussion.) There are those (e.g., some think tanks) who conclude that all privatization is superior and those (e.g., public sector labor unions) who disdain private sector involvement. This then becomes a debate over *who does it better*.

A simple example of privatization is the sale of municipal assets to the private sector. One might expect a municipality on the verge of insolvency to have already sold off its discretionary assets and terminated its optional activities. The proposed sale of a subsidized municipal golf course by a city struggling to maintain public safety services has the advantages of stopping the financial hemorrhaging from the golf course operations and providing an influx of funds that could be used to retire debt or restore financial reserves. Yet, even with so much to be gained, terminating such an activity is not easy. It is common for municipalities to battle deficits while continuing to subsidize optional activities. A city that tries to divest itself of an asset, service, or activity will encounter an unusual variety of challenges.

On one occasion, I had to curtail evaluating options to sell city-owned golf courses and land upon discovering deed restrictions that prevented the land from being subdivided or used for non-recreational purposes. Such restrictions can depress the value of the land to potential buyers or prevent the sale to a private entity. Then there is the predictable resistance from the residents who use the facilities and will have to travel farther for their leisure. Even more intense objections may come from those who are accustomed to

---

[1] David Osborne and Ted Gaebler, *Reinventing Government: How the Entrepreneurial Spirit Is Transforming the Public Sector* (Reading: Addison-Wesley, 1992), 47.

having a subsidized buffer zone between their homes and other residential developments.

Regardless of the legitimacy of the protests, an intensely focused group of dissenters raises the political costs, thereby reducing the appeal of such proposals. If the sale has any impact on current city employees or on the number of union-represented positions, the labor union will want (or may have already negotiated the right) to influence the outcome. Under pressure, it is easier to weather another year of golf course subsidy than to take on a distasteful battle. *Easier*, so long as there are funds available.

The vast inventory of assets under the control of the city organization will not yield many options to divest—at least not expeditiously. In addition to deed restrictions, outstanding bond pledges and legal restrictions associated with assets bought with federal and state grants impede the sale of municipal assets. Those who are unaccustomed to working with municipal real estate holdings are often surprised to learn of these constraints.

The contracting of utility operations, such as water or wastewater, is a popular form of privatization. Such contracts are announced as dramatic changes to the municipal utility. Some of the visible operating changes may be considerable as compared to the way the municipality had been operating. And such arrangements take a great deal of upfront work and negotiations to consummate. But fundamental elements of the municipal monopoly remain. In effect, the structure of utility service delivery changes from that of a government monopoly operating with municipal employees to that of a government monopoly overseeing privately contracted operations. A municipality retains ultimate responsibility for its utility operations regardless of how much financial risk it successfully transfers to the private operator. Further, in all such arrangements, the municipality assumes contract risk—i.e., the risk associated with the failure of the private contractor to meet its obligations.

Critics of outsourcing point to the impact on displaced workers, whose municipal jobs are converted into lower paid private sector jobs. (This objection contradicts the labor unions' claim that private sector compensation exceeds that of the public sector.) But if a displaced city worker accepts a lower paid position with a private contractor under an outsourcing arrangement, it is either because the city paid more than the worker's skills are worth or the worker chose not to pursue a position that is reflective of his or her higher worth. If the city pays more than the market value for a worker, the additional compensation comes at the expense of the taxpayers or ratepayers of all classes who then pay a premium for the services they receive. A municipal employer does not increase the value of an employee's work by paying more than that work is worth.

In some jurisdictions, the concern over worker impact results in stipulations imposed on the outsourcing contractors. The contractors must then comply with wage requirements and a host of other labor provisions that resemble the internal personnel policies of the municipal organization. In such cases, the advantages of shedding the financial burden that the municipality has taken on through its labor contracts and personnel practices are negated by placing those same burdens on the private contractors.

When city leaders grapple with insolvency, it is natural to fixate on short-term financial performance. From that perspective, buying one more year of solvency through the quick sale of a city asset—or converting future city revenues into cash via a utility operating contract in the name of privatization—looks like success. But this is nothing more than the year-to-year survival approach.

Sometimes public–private partnerships are categorized as *privatization*. A public–private partnership can refer to any cooperative agreement or collaboration between a government agency and a private company. Municipalities are attracted to these arrangements for large construction projects because they can use the private company to perform work that public agencies cannot carry out efficiently under a local government operating structure. Procurement, project management, and cost-containment, for example, are much easier for a private company to shoulder.

These cooperative arrangements raise the same issues as those in the utility operating contracts. How much control is the municipality willing to give up, given its responsibility and accountability? Again, the municipality cannot obtain the advantages it seeks from the private sector without relinquishing control and assuming contract risk. I believe a deeper question is raised by the fact that the municipality is sufficiently ill-equipped to undertake the activity, yet it retains involvement and control. I cannot resolve that question here, but I can point out that it is far from clear that a municipality is an efficacious conductor of large-scale construction projects or that it becomes proficient simply by tapping into private sector expertise.

The strategic use of privatization expressed in *Reinventing Government* has proven to be elusive. Outsourcing is straightforward when it is executed on a small scale and there is no one in the municipal organization qualified to do the work. But large-scale privatization (e.g., utility plant operations) requires a sustained effort to clearly establish the financial benefits, resolve political and labor objections (often one and the same), and execute. Many such operating contracts are better than the arrangements they replaced. But after years of operating as a monopoly utility with municipally managed personnel, productivity standards are difficult to establish with confidence.

The new contract will solve some problems and transfer some financial risk, but it will not alter the underlying municipal ownership or the implications of such ownership.

Privatization will continue to be a nonsolution until cities pause their preoccupation with the *form* of the service or activity (i.e., the details of *how* these activities are executed) in favor of resolving the *substance* (i.e., *what* is being executed vis-a-vis the local government's powers). Municipalities need to authenticate the basis for their involvement. Debates over whether private or public *does it better* distract from the fundamental question: What is the proper scope of the municipal organization?

Regionalization: Consolidation and Shared Services

If the obstacles to long-term success via privatization are formidable, then those associated with regionalization are impregnable.

Shared services and cooperative arrangements between public agencies are widely used, especially among small agencies. Contracting with the local county sheriff's office for police services is usually more cost effective than operating a small police department. Joint powers authorities and special districts allow for utility and other services to be provided across municipal jurisdictions.

But if consolidation of local agencies were a workable financial tactic to achieve economies of scale and eliminate the redundant overhead associated with administering multiple agencies, there should have been more such activity during the recessions of the early 1990s and early 2000s, as well as in the years following the 2007 Great Recession. I would also expect there to be more consolidations in the current environment.

Several factors explain why we do not see more efforts to combine municipal services strategically. First, political bodies are reluctant to cede territory or influence. This sentiment is reinforced by constituents who favor continued local control—or perceived local control—over the subject services and activities. The resulting status quo bias discourages proactive efforts to combine city operations or services with those of another municipality, despite clear financial advantages.

Then there is the issue of what specific range of services and corresponding service delivery model are being combined. The attention that managers devote to addressing political barriers distracts from the opportunity to assess whether the services should continue in the same form or continue at all. Combining unnecessary activities only sustains them. Similarly, regionalizing a tired service delivery model ensures that the inefficiencies will simply move to a larger stage. I have seen such a scenario unfold in proposals to consolidate fire services. When obtaining cooperation from stakeholders (i.e., both agencies and their respective labor unions), no one seriously challenges the status quo scope of activity or the traditional service delivery methods. Meanwhile, the labor unions want assurance that the arrangement will not result in a loss of employees whom it represents. At some point, the proposal either collapses because the financial benefit will be meager or it succeeds in order to save political face. If it succeeds, it will be in a form devoid of the benefits of economies of scale, redesign of work processes, and more efficient personnel deployment. Either way, there is little to show for the time and effort.

When political bodies insist on retaining control over a consolidation arrangement, they negotiate a contractual agreement (e.g., cooperative agreement, intergovernmental agreement, etc.) or formally establish a separate public agency (e.g., joint powers authority, intergovernmental alliance, emergency response organization, etc.) to administer the succeeding activity or service. Activities under such arrangements can be as diverse as streetlight maintenance, geographical information systems, bond financing, insurance pools, groundwater management, etc. Although the contractual agreements are flexible in their administrative requirements, they still must be managed. Meanwhile, joint powers authorities and intergovernmental agencies are legal entities that require by-laws, open meetings, and financial reporting (i.e., the administrative overhead of running a public agency).

Just in California, there are more than 1,500 active joint powers authorities that operate in addition to countless interagency services agreements. As with less formal arrangements, such cooperative agreements are not legally or technically difficult to manage or terminate. But so long as such agreements are active, agency staff must tend to the added layer of financial, recordkeeping, and legal requirements. Also, because these cooperative agencies have a lower public profile than their respective municipal members, they tend to obscure the full scope of activity undertaken by local government.

Those who believe that the current system is wasteful, clunky, and filled with redundancies are correct. But those who suggest that there is little to be gained from consolidations are also correct. Economies of scale, reduced redundancies, and interagency cooperation are only worthwhile pursuits *if* the right activities are undertaken in the right way.

Community Engagement and Budget Participation

Over the past few decades, *community engagement* has become an integral part of the local government decision-making process. Municipal staff reports sometimes require a declaration that staff conducted outreach to the community in connection with proposed city actions. Such outreach includes communications with businesses about street closures, solicitation of residents' feedback on development proposals, and public budget information sessions. In the meantime, technology has supplied new opportunities for budget outreach.

But despite city officials' invitations and encouragement, few residents participate in the budgeting process. Even when residents do attend the information sessions, it is unclear what counts as participation. If he attends one session? If she speaks? If they take a survey? And what if the resident does not grasp what is presented? City officials themselves struggle to keep up with all of the information that is relevant to the budgeting process. In the end, it does not really matter. Two types of residents attend public budget sessions: the familiar people (who are already engaged based on a specific interest such as pension costs or environmental issues) and those residents whom budget staff will never see again. But I do not think residents' lack of engagement is a consequence of their rational or irrational apathy. The traditional budgeting process eludes productive understanding and exchange. And the quality of the process is not improved by expanding the number of participants.

The rock bottom experience for the few engaged residents is afforded by the online budget simulator. Unlike an airplane simulator—which has a functional counterpart in real life—the budget simulator is the computer application that shares the budget manager's pain with everyone. In some cities, residents can visit the city's website and assume the role of budget manager in an interactive setting. These residents can change annual spending between categories—e.g., police, fire, infrastructure, library, recreation, and general government support functions—so long as the budget is balanced in the end. In other words, now it is the residents who face the intractable riddle of whether $100,000 is best spent on police protection, roof repair to a city building, or recreation programs—or if it should be kept for the future. Sometimes, there is no option to save for the future. One budget simulator instructs users to spend their *entire* allotted budget without even the possibility to save money. (To be fair to the subject city, the rules associated with this model were established by a local nonprofit organization.)[2]

Regardless of the rules of the budget simulator, managing the city's activities does not reduce to turning dials linked to financial inputs. Managing the organization via financial inputs is the ineffective scheme that performance budgeting sought to overcome. One can neither convey coherent information nor extract useful information from such a process. The budget simulator manifests what performance budgeting properly disparaged as "budget as a math game"—a realm in which the decision-maker is tortured by zero-sum tradeoffs.

When residents want to influence the city's activities, they do not patiently follow the budget development through the public information sessions or partake in online budget games. Such residents show up at final budget hearings. They may come in support of a new program (e.g., park enhancement), or they may seek the preservation of programs (e.g., library, youth, senior, etc.) that the city organization is readying to reduce or curtail.

Many cities are not discouraged by the meager interest of residents in the budgeting process. Some such cities have gone as far as to adopt *participatory budgeting* whereby groups of residents oversee the programming of a designated piece of the city's budget.[3] Although the city council retains final authority over the organization's spending, this activity includes more residents in the process of deciding city spending.

What is seen: A group of residents meets and conducts a process to decide how a designated amount of city funds is to be spent. The funds can either be special funds (e.g., federal grants), other restricted funds, or a portion of the city's general fund. The focus is on the fact that people who would otherwise have little or no role in city spending take part in the decision. Through a prescribed process, participants can suggest new city projects. Then they can approve projects that were either developed through the participatory budgeting process or recommended by city staff.

What is unseen: The real, but disregarded impact of what is forgone by spending the subject funds—i.e., what would have occurred, but now cannot occur, because these funds are not available for another use.

---

[2] "2018 People's Budget Report," Committee for a Better New Orleans, accessed May 20, 2021, from https://cbno.org/site/wp-content/uploads/2018-Peoples-Budget-Report.pdf.

[3] Alana Semuels, "The City That Gave Its Residents $3 Million," *The Atlantic*, November 6, 2014, https://www.theatlantic.com/business/archive/2014/11/the-city-that-gave-its-residents-3-million/382348/.

In this case, the unseen appears undramatic, even insignificant. Perhaps most participatory budget processes yield decisions very similar to those that the city council would have made anyway. But what is significant is that offering parts of the budget for disposal by specified groups expands the organization's scope of activity. Thus financial stability gives way to a satellite spending process.

Some ventures into participatory budgeting are touted as a civics lesson for students. But we should not be teaching anyone that a municipality improves its budgeting process by creating new avenues for spending.

More and Better Information: Data and Transparency

In an input-oriented environment, more is better for the city organization: To provide more services, the city requires more money, more staff, and more budget participants. This approach carries over to municipalities' management of public access to data and financial information. If some information is good, then more is better. Under this approach, the key to public trust and better budget decision-making is the proactive dissemination of maximum financial information.

The internet, cheap data storage, and improved data retrieval tools have united to make it possible for municipalities of all sizes to provide public access to detailed financial data. What began with posting financial statements and budgets online has progressed into *interactive access to data.* One can meander through years of historical financial information, zoom in on underlying data, and create unlimited charts and graphs. Data can be isolated by timeframe, by department, by fund, by expense group, revenue type, etc. When a municipality's antiquated financial system is insufficient to deliver online access, third-party applications cover the gap.

Since financial transparency tools arrived on the scene several years ago, a vast volume of city financial data is readily available on city website portals. Yet this data has not increased the level of public understanding. Nor has it improved the quality of municipal decision-making.

Whenever I entered a local government organization to aid with or review its budget, I found the outwardly facing transparency tools to be fruitless. Even when extraordinary resources are dedicated to annotating and providing relevant background information, the utility of these tools is limited. The historical information is only helpful if one understands the full range of municipal operations, accounting policies (there are many options that affect how activities are reported), and any unusual financial events. It does not take long to reach diminishing returns on the time spent pursuing endless data on a city's financial portal.

But the residents should not feel marginalized. The embarrassing secret is that most municipalities do not manage their financial accounting and budgeting systems in a manner that is *internally transparent*. By this I mean that most managers inside the organization have a limited, fragmented understanding of the organization's finances. Even the internal financial systems and forecasting tools are severely limited as a one-stop source from which one can understand the organization's financial and budgeting activities. In the same pattern of garbage in / garbage out, an internal lack of financial comprehensiveness will only propagate confusion when transmitted via a portal to those outside the organization.

Data is not information. And information out of context is not useful. Without a coherent framework, a local government organization cannot use its data to assemble financial information in a context that is useful for its own decision-making. Until it does that, its data—however transparently and dynamically presented as information—will not be useful to those outside the organization. And access to financial data is not what prevents municipalities from performing better financially. Municipal officials and residents already have sufficient information with which to address the root of the financial problems that their organizations face.

Residents and businesses have every right to be informed about what their local government organizations are doing and how municipal officials make decisions. Open meetings, public records requests, and transparency portals play a positive role in local government. However, when there is underlying decision-making dysfunction, these transparency tools do more to supply cover for poor decisions, financial and nonfinancial, than they do to support good ones.

Other Financial Tactics: Policies and Diagnostics

Whether real or imagined, the pressure on cities to do *something* during financial decline inspires a host of solutions from many sources. While the extroverts extoll the merits of community engagement, the introverts work on financial policies and financial health assessments. I am in the latter category, so I spent quite a bit of time developing and promoting the nationally endorsed best practices and compiling numbers for evaluations of organizational financial health. The management in these organizations believed that if the municipality operated with sound policies, embraced best financial practices, and monitored key financial metrics—the organization would thrive. Sadly, none of that work affected the organization's financial course. I later reflected on whether the attempts at implementing better policies was simply too little, too late or if there was a better explanation for the failures.

According to the GFOA, "Financial policies are used by a governing board and executive management to set the baseline standards for how the organization will be managed financially."[4] Accordingly, such policies provide a structured approach to the decision-making process from a financial perspective. Financial policies provide guidance on issues that include investment management, reserve balances, bond issuance, pension funding, capital asset management, financial reporting, etc.

As with the budget, financial policies operate *within* the decision-making approach of the organization. A bond issuance policy can provide guidance on and clarify the financial implications of selling bonds, but it cannot help with the evaluation of whether the proposed project is proper or whether the city organization should be incurring debt at all. A policy that limits the spending of one-time revenues to one-time expenses sounds sensible—for example, using the sale of a municipal asset to fund a public construction project. But it is not helpful if the organization disregards other impacts of the project. Municipal officials cannot segregate *fiscal management* from *organizational management*. Financial policies cannot overcome the organization's decision-making approach or the values that sustain that approach.

As city officials watch the waning financial condition of cities nationwide, they seek usable information with which to gauge their own city's status. Is the organization financially secure? Or is it in a financial death spiral? Prompted chiefly by concerns stemming from municipalities' commitments to retirees and accumulation of debt, watch groups have been monitoring the financial commitments of local and state governments for many years. Recently, the California State Auditor began to release financial health ratings of cities throughout the state. Meanwhile, several diagnostic tools are available that permit cities to perform their own financial assessments. These tools use measurements of available cash, operating result trends, fixed costs and commitments, and other available financial information to evaluate the organization's financial health and identify key risk factors.

However, the financial diagnostic tools suffer from several technical and practical issues. First, the audited financial data on which much of the analysis depends is largely outdated and only refreshed annually. In the case of a

[4] "Financial Policies," Government Finance Officers Association, accessed May 20, 2021, from https://gfoa.org/materials/financial-policies-book.

struggling city that is delinquent in completing its annual financial audit, the information is not just tardy, but obsolete. But even when the financial audit is timely, the measurement of employee retirement commitments, usually one of the largest obligations, depends upon pension and medical benefit data that lags by one or more years. Thus, the financial assessment is based on information at least twelve-to-eighteen months old.

Exacerbating the lack of timeliness is the lack of completeness. Because it is unusual for a municipality to maintain a current evaluation of the condition of all of the assets (e.g., buildings, streets, parks, etc.) under its control, the cost of deferred maintenance and assets in need of replacement must be estimated. Thus, the financial assessment takes on the quality of loose speculation rather than of a methodical calculation of financial health.

For a city organization in a financial tailspin, the resulting information may provide municipal officials with a different perspective on some areas—e.g., available cash, debt, ongoing obligations. And the old and incomplete information and estimates do not necessarily generate results that are grossly misleading. However, the analysis will not inform the leadership of more than it already knows—or more than what it should know from its routine financial management. If a city has a persistent financial deficit or is otherwise on a course that could result in insolvency, its tenuous condition is evident in the budgeting process and further revealed in the annual financial reporting. The preparation of an alternative set of financial information distracts from the discussions and actions that should arise from the organization's core financial planning and reporting activities.

As with other nonsolutions, the lack of effectiveness of this tool goes beyond technical limitations and execution. It is beyond the scope of financial health diagnostics to challenge service-delivery methods that drive the organization's spending. Yet, a municipality's controllable costs are embedded in its service-delivery system. Further, the tools do not differentiate the city resources that are committed to activities that can *only* be performed by the city from those resources committed to activities for which there are alternatives. Thus, the financial health diagnostics do not help the city council identify its full range of options.

The benefits of municipal financial assessments are largely confined to those outside the organization (e.g., state auditors, local reporters, and industry journalists). The compilation of financial diagnostic information does not *cause* municipal decision-making to become data driven. Nor does it address how decision-makers can use the information effectively. Even the most current, complete, and accurate financial data will not overcome an inadequate decision-making approach.

New Paradigms for Decision-Making

Since the Great Recession, the focus of the Government Finance Officers Association (GFOA) has evolved from financial policies, measures, and metrics to the broader perspective of how local governments should make financial decisions. In its presentation of a new approach to financial sustainability, the GFOA states:

> A popular answer to the financial challenges of local governments is to run government "like a business". This prescription does offer value, such as emphasizing efficiency in service provision and measurement of government performance. However, it is not fully satisfactory because it ignores the fundamental difference between government and business: government is a public organization while a business is private."[5]

Certainly, the aim to run government "like a business" has proven unsatisfactory. But the "fundamental difference" deserves a deeper account than "government is a public organization while a business is private." Government is a public organization because it is the local legislative and enforcement authority. Thus, the GFOA misses an opportunity to recognize a key factor to consider in deciding what a local government organization *should* and *should not* do.

The GFOA proceeds to point out that "[t]he goals of public organizations are often more ambiguous."[6] True enough. But isn't this something that we should strive to fix rather than tolerate? The goals of government are only ambiguous because municipal officials permit them to be so. The GFOA's observation highlights the critical need for municipal officials to define their organization's goals with delimitation and precision.

Unfortunately, the GFOA concedes the ambiguity of governments' goals. It then proceeds to build its financial sustainability approach on the government leaders' need for a scheme for making decisions in this ambiguous context that requires the agreement of several diverse parties. This new paradigm follows from "the tragedy of the commons."

In short, the tragedy of the commons is a situation in which independent entities share access to a limited common resource, and they risk depleting

---

[5] Shane Kavanagh, *The New Financial Sustainability Framework* (Chicago: Government Finance Officers Association, 2017), 4, https://gfoaorg.cdn.prismic.io/gfoaorg/78f17413-bf27-4ce6-8d0b-64993c4776ba_Financial+Sustainability+White+Paper-v2_0.pdf.

[6] Shane Kavanagh, *The New Financial Sustainability Framework* (Chicago: Government Finance Officers Association, 2017), 4, https://gfoaorg.cdn.prismic.io/gfoaorg/78f17413-bf27-4ce6-8d0b-64993c4776ba_Financial+Sustainability+White+Paper-v2_0.pdf.

that resource if they do not cooperate effectively. A classic example is that of unrestricted fisheries. In such an environment, recreational fishers and commercial fishing businesses have no incentive to limit their independent activity. So everyone proceeds to catch fish without regard for long-term impacts. This becomes *tragic* when the aggregation of these independent pursuits depletes the fish stock to the detriment of all. The GFOA likens this scenario to the local government and its financial resources:

> A government and its financial resources are commonly owned by all citizens of the government. Further, each stakeholder of the government has an incentive to extract resources from the public budget. Stakeholders often find themselves "in competition" with others to get resources, so therefore try to get as much as possible lest they lose their resources to others.[7]

If unchecked or mismanaged, the tragedy manifests in the deterioration of the financial health of the organization. The GFOA uses this model to propose leadership, long-term visioning, and communication strategies as a means to managing *the commons*—i.e., the local government's resources.[8]

But municipal resources are not a natural phenomenon. A city's resources come exclusively from private (i.e., non-common) sources. Taxation is a forced *commonizing* of that which was previously not common. Thus, local government resources are not comparable to air, waterways, unclaimed grazing land, and open fisheries.

It is true that some of the visible stakeholders (e.g., labor unions, developers, environmentalists, department heads, local businesses, and civic groups) may seek to extract resources from the organization. But politically outnumbered and outshouted are the silent residents and businesses whose resources were extracted to fund the organization. Likewise, there is no voice for those residents who do not wish to use the power of local government to dispose of resources conscripted from their neighbors. Also unheard and unseen are the future residents and businesses who inherit the ravaged commons.

When the commons cannot be subdivided—as is the case with air and open waterways—regional government oversight is needed to protect residents, businesses, and their property. But why would anyone create or

---

[7] Shane Kavanagh, *The New Financial Sustainability Framework* (Chicago: Government Finance Officers Association, 2017), 4, https://gfoaorg.cdn.prismic.io/gfoaorg/78f17413-bf27-4ce6-8d0b-64993c4776ba_Financial+Sustainability+White+Paper-v2_0.pdf.

[8] Shane Kavanagh, *The New Financial Sustainability Framework* (Chicago: Government Finance Officers Association, 2017), 4, https://gfoaorg.cdn.prismic.io/gfoaorg/78f17413-bf27-4ce6-8d0b-64993c4776ba_Financial+Sustainability+White+Paper-v2_0.pdf.

maintain commons unnecessarily? The lesson of the tragedy of the commons is that when *everyone* owns something, *no one* owns it; therefore, no one has an interest in the long-term consequences. In the case of fisheries, grazing land, and some contained waterways, the tragedy and the commons have been resolved by establishing property rights. The real tragedy of the commons is that there are too many commons—or, more precisely, too many contrived commons. Where city government could have been used positively to protect the interests of residents and businesses through the mediation of property rights, it sustains and expands the tragedy.

Where does this approach leave city leaders in their endeavor to manage the organization's resources? The paradigm has shifted from the pricing of scarce city services to the prisoner's dilemma. Can it get worse?

The Limits of Municipal Bankruptcy

Yes, it can get worse. Bankruptcy is the visible crash of the commons. It is the nonsolution that chooses itself. Cities do not file for bankruptcy protection because they want to. None of the bankruptcy attorneys recommend it. On the contrary, I have listened to bankruptcy attorneys admonish cities about the costs and limitations of municipal bankruptcy. The features of municipal bankruptcy are vastly different from and the results less predictable than those of personal and commercial bankruptcies. But imagine a financial hole so overwhelmingly large that to resolve it requires concessions from bond holders (or bond insurers), other creditors, retirees, and current employees that cannot be obtained through voluntary negotiations or mediation.

Bankruptcy comes at an enormous cost to the city organization and to those who rely upon it. In addition to the expense of hiring specialized attorneys and consultants, the internal resources of the organization are either consumed by the activities associated with the bankruptcy or paralyzed by the uncertainty of the outcome. Whatever level of productivity the organization may have had is diminished. The downward financial spiral that prompted the bankruptcy continues during the process of making the decision to file and throughout the months of bankruptcy proceedings.

As with the other nonsolutions, there are genuine issues that bankruptcy can address. A city organization can be overextended with respect to contractual obligations. Sufficient resources may not be available to fulfill the commitments associated with labor contracts, debt (e.g., bonds and loans), and commitments to other creditors. But the benefits of municipal bankruptcy are limited. The bankruptcy court does not have the authority to set aside city charter provisions, regardless of the role that those provisions may play in the municipality's financial degradation. It can take years after a bankruptcy to successfully change a city charter. Even then, ambitious charter changes are discouraged because they have the potential to jeopardize the entire ballot proposal.

After enduring the cost and pain of their bankruptcies, bankrupt cities emerge with the *same* city charter, the *same* organizational chart, the *same* array of boards and commissions, the *same* mission, vision, and goals—i.e., the same fundamentals that paved the road to insolvency. Thus, post-bankruptcy, there is no reliable safeguard from an eventual repeat.

Additional Tax Revenues

With seemingly nowhere else to go, taxes—new or expanded sales taxes, property parcel taxes, utility users taxes, hotel taxes, etc.—emerge as the only viable solution. Some residents see the solution as straightforward: simply cut the fat, reduce spending, and run more efficiently. But when city councilmembers are elected on such platforms, their contrary perspective and votes do not influence the financial course. Without a positive vision or specific solutions, there is little inspiration. So the organization pursues additional tax revenues.

New taxes often add organizational and financial tension. Proponents of new programs are pitted against those who prefer that the new funds are dedicated to preserving current city services. In municipal organizations, new revenues are usually committed at least once before they are collected. The labor units and community advocates who aided with the passing of a tax measure will want to influence the disposition of the tax revenues. These *hidden commissions* on the taxes are devastating to cities that are already financially stretched.

It may seem presumptuous to assert that additional taxes are *always* a nonsolution and that their use amounts to an admission that the organization is in year-to-year survival. But if one considers how local governments develop proposed tax increases, this perspective is easier to understand.

Although a city may start out with a target tax increase in mind to resolve an assumed deficit, it does not take long for the target to move to that which the city officials believe can be imposed successfully. Such is the nature of taxes. If the target tax increase is higher than what city officials believe can be imposed successfully, the target will not be realized. If the city officials believe that they can impose a tax that exceeds the target level, their focus shifts to maximizing services. In the end, regardless of whether the proposed tax increase is higher or lower than the target increase, it is not tied to the cost of any specific array of services. Local taxes thus gravitate to the maximum tax that the city leadership believes can be imposed successfully.

Community surveys test the viability of potential tax proposals among those most likely to vote. Specifically, the city officials want to know the conditions under which sufficient votes can be secured. For example: Would the voters pass a $100 per year parcel (property) tax to maintain the open hours for the library? Would the voters pass a 0.25% increase in sales tax to maintain the number of police officers and firefighters? Would the voters pass a 0.50% increase in sales tax to increase the number of police officers and firefighters? This approach is consistent with the model described in *The Price of Government*: "By 'the price of government,' we mean the amount of purchasing power a community is willing to commit to its governments."[9]

Because city officials' evaluation of the maximum that local voters will approve (or tolerate) has no firm tie to the city's commitments, a new tax yields a variety of results. A sales tax increase enacted in response to an economic slowdown that takes effect just as the economy recovers can add to unanticipated tax revenues for which the city organization has not identified a use. A similar tax increase established for the purpose of maintaining or expanding service levels that takes effect simultaneously with an economic slowdown is unlikely to deliver on its promise. Nor can city officials guarantee that a tax increase enacted in stable economic times will support the level of intended services into the future.

Regardless of the particular outcome, the city organization's commitments and spending trends eventually catch up, and it is time for new community surveys to test what the taxpayers will bear. This is the cycle of expanding taxes that perseveres. And it is why additional tax revenues are a nonsolution.

Thoughts and Prayers

There are certainly some financial remedies of which I am not aware. Perhaps more are forthcoming. But as local government services deteriorate, the recycling of nonsolutions is the dominant trend. My positive solution, presented later, is intended to shift city decisions from those that sustain confusion,

[9] David Osborne and Peter Hutchinson, *The Price of Government: Getting the Results We Need in an Age of Permanent Fiscal Crisis* (New York: Basic Books, 2004), 41.

frustration, and scarcity to those that promote clear actions that are consistent with a healthy relationship among the city organization, its residents, and business owners.

A nadir. Several years ago, a city conducted a three-day prayer and fast amid one of its desperate financial panics. Where the call for prayer and fast was embraced, the sentiment expressed was: "Why not?"[10] Many poor municipal decisions originate from *why not*. In evaluating solutions, or any local government actions, it is important to maintain one's focus on that which is positively compelling—the answer to *why*. What does the proposed solution or action accomplish? A solution that develops from the expectation that any action is better than nothing should only be expected to consume time.

The limited and elusive benefits of these nonsolutions constitute a cumulative alarm that should wake up municipalities to the need to settle the issue of *what the organization should do* before indulging in debates over details of *how it does it*. Without this step, there will be no basis for better budgeting; technology and work process improvements will be rudderless; contracting and outsourcing strategies will be hollow; the residents in the community will not be able to properly engage; data will continue to have no useful context; transparency will be meaningless; financial policies will be ineffective; financial health diagnostics will be pointless—and praying and fasting sessions will appear to be the only alternative to a perpetual cycle of tax increases.

I have criticized conventional budgeting solutions and financial remedies for failing to address what a city (or any municipality) *should be doing*, i.e., its proper scope. But the issue is deeper. In order to evaluate the organization's proper scope, one must first know what that organization is. No budgeting methodology or fiscal remedy can overcome an amorphous organization.

City governments need a real budgeting solution. But first, city officials, residents, and budget managers need to know *what is a city government*. That is what I turn to next.

[10] Diana Fishlock, "If Prayer for Harrisburg Helps, Local Clergy Say 'Why Not'?" PennLive, June 23, 2011, accessed June 19, 2021, from https://pennlive.com/midstate/2011/06/if_prayer_for_the_health_of_ha.html.

7

Discovering the Value of City Government

My Journey

In my three decades in municipal government, I never had a conversation about what a city government is. I never avoided such a discussion. The topic never arose. I am not sure whether people thought that the answer was obvious or the question irrelevant.

From time to time, I worked with employees who appeared to be lost, unable to follow what the organization was doing or what it should be doing. In retrospect, they *were* lost. They were lost because they were counting on the organization to have something that it did not. The organization was missing something. Despite its grand vision, the organization did not know what it was or what value it had to offer the residents. The organization was lost.

Other employees found ways to cope with the nebulous nature of city hall. They focused on their operational assignments and department goals. But a finance director and budget manager cannot so readily avoid the consequences of an organization that has a unique type of identity crisis—an organization that has *no* identity.

I now take you through my discovery of the value of city government, what city government is, and how the human community established in government comports with other human communities, personal and commercial. I then build on these relationships to present a framework for evaluating the various activities of local government.

M. Moses, *The Municipal Financial Crisis*,
https://doi.org/10.1007/978-3-030-87836-8_7

Before I began working in municipal government, I had not interacted much with local government; nor had I thought deeply about its activities. I had never visited a city hall, nor had I watched a public meeting. At first, I carried with me some typical biases about government workers shared by many in the private sector. I thought such workers to be somewhat unambitious and indifferent. It did not take long after joining a municipality to see that local government teems with intelligent, hardworking, committed employees.

I also held some broad views related to government, particularly with respect to its involvement in commercial activities. For example, I did not think government should take on *anything* that a private business could do. But I did not believe this because I thought that government was inherently incompetent or evil. Rather, I did not see profit as evil. To the contrary, I saw profit as the measure of economic value—value that can only come from a free exchange in a market. Before my time in government, I worked with several private businesses. The value that they provided to their customers was measured by profit—profit that was only guaranteed so long as these businesses delivered demonstrable value.

There is a clear linkage between freedom to innovate and trade, the profit that arises when this trade is successful, and the outcomes from this activity that we value. This value appears in the technology we enjoy, the buildings we see and use, and the inventions that save us our most important value, our time. And there is a clear link between government and these values. It is government that enables free exchange through its protection of people, property, and trade.

If the role of government as protector sounds incidental, imagine starting a business in the absence of such protection. A successful business requires the ability to plan, produce, and trade. Government is integral to a social and legal infrastructure that enables businesses to make decisions and take actions over time. Businesses can perform these activities knowing that they can produce and trade free from physical interruption. And such businesses enjoy the benefits of successful production and trade in the form of profit. The existence and sustenance of contract law, protected and upheld by government, supports all of these productive activities.

As I entered municipal government, I was also unconvinced that the authority of government is needed in charitable and other noncommercial undertakings. If an activity or a service is important to a community (e.g., serving meals to seniors, addressing non-lifestyle homelessness, offering youth sports), I thought that it would be initiated, supported, and managed by those most interested. Such individuals and groups can design their organizations around their vision and appeal to donors who share that vision. Just as profit measures economic value, the satisfaction of personal values measures charitable and other noncommercial activities.

Local government cannot compete with the passion, creativity, or versatility of a private charity or a nonprofit organization. It can only compete with the funding of such activities by drawing on the source of such funding—private sector production. But government has a positive role to play. Just as government protects entrepreneurs through its protection of property rights and trade, it likewise protects champions of charity and their beneficiaries.

I sometimes heard proposals to blend government and the private sector in order to get the *best of both worlds*. Some people see local government as being in a unique position to orchestrate or facilitate initiatives that can benefit from combining what government and the private sector each have to offer. The private sector is recognized for its innovation, creativity, productivity, and passion. Meanwhile, local government has financial resources, personnel capacity, and legislative authority. Such proposals can lead to the privatization arrangements discussed previously as well as to cooperative arrangements with charitable organizations. My initial apprehension regarding such suggestions has only been reinforced over the years.

After having spent substantial time in both of these worlds, I still fail to see any merit to these arrangements. Other than as a source of supplies, materials, and technical expertise, a municipality does not need the private sector to perform its governmental functions. And whenever a commercial or charitable firm proposed to use the powers of local government to supplement the conduct of its business, that firm was compensating for its inability to achieve its goals through persuasion. Such firms wanted to exploit the government organization's resources—resources appropriated from local residents. What else would a private firm have to gain from the government besides an unfair favor? The way to achieve the best of both worlds is to understand what each world is—i.e., the nature of the private sector, the nature of government, and their respective requirements. Then we can establish the proper relationship between these worlds.

Nor was I ever enthusiastic about government-initiated legislation of adult behavior beyond that which is required to protect residents from the physical threat of others. Such government intervention invites conflict among those who want to use the power of government to impose their own ideas on others. When a local government acts in this manner, it stimulates community polarization and resentment. Whether the legislation takes the form of vice laws (e.g., massage ordinances), banning sales (e.g., flavored cigarettes), or outlawing certain packaging materials (e.g., styrofoam), such restrictions compromise free association within the community.

The legislation of behavior is a form of overriding the residents' judgment. But the residents' judgment is basic and essential to their flourishing. It is how they choose their values and goals. It is how they choose their friends, jobs, hobbies, and where to live. None of these values has meaning—or the potential to be realized—when one's judgment is impeded or preempted.

Cities sometimes frame issues as: if the city does not do *x*, then no one will do it. Or if the city does not require *y*, then no one will do the "right" thing. But if *x* is so important, why wouldn't the residents support it voluntarily? And if *y* is incontestably good, why wouldn't residents do it as a natural exercise of their own judgment? Cities can use their powers to intervene, as they do with municipal monopolies. But how far does the ability to intervene or compel advance a community that, left on its own, will not make rational choices? Such a community has a problem that no government can solve.

A community incapable of making good decisions and exercising good judgment would not establish a government to protect residents' ability to make decisions. Residents that establish such a government with such a purpose advance their autonomy and their freedom to act on their judgment in the pursuit of their goals. The alternative to government intervention is not chaos and decline, but freedom and flourishing. The flourishing of residents is lost when local government hampers their freedom to engage in the autonomous actions by which their goal pursuit and flourishing is enabled.

Meanwhile, you cannot ask violent criminals to willingly report to jail. And not all civil disputes among residents and businesses can be resolved voluntarily. Here we need local government to do what the private sector cannot. A community without a government to protect residents from criminals and resolve personal and commercial civil disputes is not a community. In the case of personal and property crimes, the community needs an objective enforcer of physical order. The alternative is vigilante justice and gang rivalry. In the case of civil disputes, the community needs an impartial arbiter with the authority to bring closure to a dispute. The alternative is mob protection and more violent clashes. The local government's legitimate authority to impose resolution to such criminal behavior and civil conflicts advances residents' freedom and autonomy.

Like many life-serving values to which we are accustomed—such as clean water, electricity, and well-stocked grocery stores—the value of government is easy to overlook as we go about our business. Just as we do not stop to consider all of the actions that must take place to stock a grocery store with food—the planning, the investment, the production, the storage, the transportation, etc.—we do not routinely stop to consider how government enables such planning, investment, production, storage, and transportation. The commodities and services that we need to survive must be produced. Likewise, government is not a natural resource.

From a certain perspective, local government makes possible our flourishing by protecting our life-serving values and activities. But our flourishing begins before that. Our flourishing begins when we establish a government that ensures our freedom to engage in such commercial and personal activities in service to our individual lives.

The value of local government is lost in the shuffle of power struggles, cronyism, unnecessary conflict, forced charity, and failed commercial ventures. The value of local government does not need to be saved or sustained. It needs to be discovered.

What Is a City Government?

What if someone were to suggest that, instead of leaping into the development of broad organizational missions and ambitious visions, city officials should first answer a more basic question—a question that almost no one ever asks …

What is a city government?

City government is not a water bill, a building permit, a business license, or an emergency service call. City government is not whatever the city government happens to be doing. City government is the institution that protects us so we can plan our days, choose our careers, and live our lives. And city government is the institution that ensures that we can move about our cities and pursue our own goals. Residents and business owners need a city government that acts, not as an end in itself, but as a means to their ends.

Communities need an authority designated to resolve conflicts among residents and businesses. Communities need that authority to apply the legislative and enforcement powers of government to define and enforce personal and property rights that ensure residents' and business owners' freedom to engage in personal and commercial activities.

This is why we establish local governments. This is why we need institutions empowered with legislative and enforcement powers. This is why we need "a human community that (successfully) claims the *monopoly of the legitimate use of physical force* within a given territory."[1]

[1] Max Weber, *From Max Weber: Essays in Sociology*, translated by H. H. Gerth and C. W. Mills (New York: Oxford University Press, 1946), 78.

The human community established in government stands in contrast to the voluntary communities of commerce and personal associations. When government acts, it acts directly or indirectly by means of force, coercion, compulsion. A government's power of force establishes certain relationships and precludes others. The voluntary sectors know that they are providing a value because they are being engaged by willing participants. A nonprofit's donors receive personal value commensurate with their donations; otherwise, there would be no reason for them to donate. A commercial business knows that its customers value its products more than what they pay; otherwise, there would be no reason for the customer to initiate the purchase. Government has no equivalent measure of transactional value. The value of government is that it protects the ability of these other values to transact unencumbered.

Consumed by the open-ended pursuit of service delivery, city officials are not in touch with why their organizations are so important to the community of residents and business owners. Every municipal organization I worked for or with was constantly trying to determine what its residents wanted—i.e., what was of value to them. If these organizations understood the source of their value to residents, they would not have struggled in vain to figure out what they should be doing. Now such agencies can move forward with confidence.

The city government's power to compel or restrict individual action is different from the economic power of businesses and residents. And the city government's power is likewise different from the power of shared values that drive nonprofits and their sponsors. A government can demand compliance. Individuals and businesses gain cooperation through persuasion. Imagine negotiating the sale of your property to the city. During the discussions, you are firmly aware that the city can invoke eminent domain. A business can fire you or set the price of its product higher than you can afford, but it cannot leave you worse off than if it had never existed. Setting aside crony-type influences—which rely upon the coordinated abuse of government powers—a business cannot legally coerce one to act, nor can it restrict voluntary associations or trade. A nonprofit organization can promote a cause to which you are opposed, but it cannot take your money to fund its goals.

However, a commercial business and nonprofit organization will be of no help to you in a dispute over property rights. Nor can they help you if you have been robbed or defrauded. Nor can they enforce nuisance laws or laws that protect you from private actions that threaten your health.

One of the lessons that I learned repeatedly throughout my career in municipal government is to have realistic expectations of what can be achieved through local powers and authority. The problem is not that municipal officials overestimate the abilities of people in the organization. Rather, they misjudge what government authority can accomplish. Local government's *comparative advantage*—to abuse the term—is that it can legally prevent market activity (whether competition or trade) and use conscripted resources to fund its activities. But there is no reason to think that this power will lead to desirable outcomes in every community endeavor, as contrasted with that which private, competitive, voluntary, laser-focused organizations can provide.

When a municipality establishes a local monopoly for the provision of water, sewer, ambulance, solid waste, transportation, etc., it prevents other potential service providers from participating in the market for that service. The organization may administer the service directly (water and sewer), via contract (e.g., solid waste hauling), or by granting permission to a local operation (e.g., bus or taxi). Regardless of the form of the service delivery, the organization asserts itself as the sole lawful purveyor. Rather than use its local powers to protect the market for the benefit of producers and consumers, it guarantees that no one can legally compete.

Occasionally, breakthrough technology and bold companies remind us of what we give up by banning competition and free exchange. Uber turned city-granted taxi monopolies on their side. Thanks to streaming technology, cable TV franchises are no longer the only source of television programming. No one knows what new technology might bring to solid waste processing that will reduce the need for hauling and centralized sewer treatment. Or when advanced water generation systems will simplify water distribution. Or when a company will produce vehicles that avert wear and tear of the streets. Unfortunately, municipalities pit themselves against these innovations when they monopolize rather than protect the delivery of local services.

Examining the nature of government in contrast to that of commercial activities is useful in explaining why municipalities struggle with defining, measuring, and setting the fees for their services. Although we speak loosely of *government services* and *municipal services*, confusing government activities with market services leads to the faulty conclusion that anything the city organization does provides an economic value. In the marketplace of goods and services, *value* is established by the buyer's willingness to make the exchange. Setting aside, for now, fee-based undertakings—e.g., recreation programs, golf courses, airports, etc.—municipal activities cannot be evaluated in the same way.

For example, mandatory fire inspections, building permit issuance, road maintenance, and library access are all exchanges that do not arise from a willing buyer and a willing seller-provider. They are funded through a combination of mandatory taxes and fees, and they are received either involuntarily (e.g., fire inspections) or voluntarily without regard to what funding was contributed (e.g., library usage). Then, when cities summarize their annual organizational accomplishments and *services provided*, they report on the number of fire inspections, building permits, miles of roads maintained, and library hours.

In the absence of a free exchange, the economic *value* to the recipients of these voluntarily consumed services (i.e., use of roads, library, or parks) cannot be established. Some cities use surveys to compensate for this information deficit. Such outreach tells the city organization what residents *want* it to do. But the survey responders do not face any direct tradeoffs. It costs these responders nothing to assign high priority to new city services or facilities. As a result, surveys and other community feedback generate yet more demands upon the city organization. Thus, such outreach clouds, not clarifies, the municipal decision-making process.

In the case of fee-based activities (e.g., golf course, airport, recreation programs, etc.), a municipal government disrupts the market in a manner that no other organization can. A city may choose not to prohibit competition outright, leaving local businesses and nonprofit organizations free to offer similar services. From the city officials' perspective, the city is not limiting or restricting voluntary activity. However, the city's presence displaces those who would otherwise pursue their livelihoods or charitable interests by offering such services. *Value exchange* is further disrupted by the city government's ability to intentionally—and sometimes unintentionally—subsidize these activities with local taxes.

City officials are not the only ones responsible for the organization's ungrounded expectations. Residents and businesses also misjudge the limitations of city government authority. Too often, they encourage city officials to take on local issues (e.g., recreation facilities, housing, community events, etc.), forgetting that all the city organization has at its disposal is legislative and taxing powers. Perhaps these constituents simply want to maximize their own benefit from the taxes they pay. In any case, the city's mission and vision propels the city council forward. City staff then spend time managing the gap between community expectations and what a city organization can deliver. This activity distracts everyone from the real value of the city organization.

Perhaps local governments engage in more than they should because city officials focus on delivering results rather than on providing the conditions for the residents and businesses to achieve their own results. For example, to support their respective downtown businesses, some cities establish business improvement districts. These districts, financed by local tax assessments, coordinate marketing campaigns and other activities intended to promote downtown commerce. But when a business owner is forced to contribute, she is denied the opportunity to use her best judgment in how to spend her marketing budget (if she even needs one). Similarly, a homeowner whose taxes subsidize recreation programs is denied the use of his resources to pay for his child's violin lessons. Residents and business owners cannot pursue their values when their judgment is overruled and their autonomy denied. By taking over private decision-making, city organizations take credit for the outcomes—even though the outcomes are worse than they would have been had the city protected rather than disrupted private decision-making.

Using local government authority to take charge of commercial or charitable activities does not establish a municipality's proficiency. Nor is there even an expectation of proficiency. As a finance director, I was not expected to know anything about the economics or business of recreation services, childcare, water and sewer utilities, road maintenance, solid waste, or any other city service or activity. I still cannot claim that any of the financial lessons I learned are transferable to private providers of any such services. Profit—the measure of successful value exchange between producer and consumer—is inapplicable to municipal fiscal management. And the relationship between a nonprofit organization and its donors is vastly different from that between a local government and taxpayers. Thus, in these municipal endeavors, there was no measure of proficiency.

Municipalities can achieve proficiency at all levels of the organization. But they need to do so the way successful organizations do so. They must delimit their activity to that for which they are suited and for which their success can be measured. Local government is suited for legislation and enforcement that protects residents and businesses. Such is the standard by which its proficiency can be measured.

It is quite possible that community members will contest the precise role that city government should play. Today, local governments often use their authority to override the free, voluntary choices of individuals. Some people think that this is a good thing, and I will examine the reasons offered for this view when I discuss the standards used by municipal officials to justify their organization's involvement. Regardless, acknowledging the nature of government is key to understanding the value of city government. It is also essential to making informed decisions, understanding the economic impacts of the organization's actions, and developing lasting financial solutions.

Evaluating and Classifying Municipal Activities

In order to guide the evaluation of the organization's scope and range of activity, municipal officials need an appropriate classification approach. Without a fact-based standard by which to classify municipal activities, local governments have no way to make sense of the hundreds of activities that they have undertaken. Past attempts to classify and prioritize municipal activities have failed because they have not incorporated the nature of government and the needs of residents and businesses in relation to that nature.

From the perspective of fulfilling the needs of residents and businesses, an activity that requires an agent of force is different from one that does not. To develop a proper scope, municipal officials must regard what force can and cannot do (i.e., it can restrict, it cannot produce) and what economic power can and cannot do (i.e., it can persuade, it cannot force).

The classification and prioritization of municipal activities are no better than the criteria used to establish them. For example, a simple distinction, often used by cities, is that of *essential and nonessential services*. As an extension, some facilities are assigned the status of essential services buildings. But such distinctions rarely provide a useful means to make budgeting or operating decisions. As we learned from the COVID-19 lockdown orders, the definition of *essential* is so vague that virtually anything can be considered essential.

When cities prioritize projects and programs, the principal criteria they use are *legal compliance* and *safety*, trailed closely by *community quality of life* (or the equivalent). The justifications for the first two are that the city must follow that which is legally required and should value safety over other considerations (e.g., cost, esthetics, synergy with other activities, etc.). The usefulness of this approach is limited because, as with essential and nonessential, the criteria used to gauge legal compliance and safety are vague. I can point out that the production of annual financial statements is legally required, but that does not help decide whether the organization should have one accountant or three, or how much it should spend on accounting software.

Priority-Driven Budgeting exposed the trappings of vague prioritization criteria. Interpreted broadly, *safety* can encompass all of the activities in police, fire, and facility maintenance. When the criterion is expanded to *health and safety*, recreation services are included. And when their role in providing shelter and information pertaining to health is weighed, libraries also survive the cut. If it cannot find a home somewhere else, *any* activity that promises a benefit to *anyone* contributes to the community's quality of life.

The quality of cities' prioritization of activities and programs is compromised, not only by ambiguous criteria, but by city officials' own reluctance to formalize the results. Declaring city priorities requires that city officials designate some activities to be less important than others. But to plainly rank one local service or activity below another risks offending the employees whose jobs are associated, residents who may benefit, and others who support the lesser undertaking. Meanwhile, the absence of definitive organizational priorities has practical consequences. For example, if a city must furlough or lay off workers, it cannot just target library staff. It must spread the pain across every department—even if this means, say, harming the water department's ability to serve its customers.

As long as city officials pursue priority setting in terms of figuring out relative importance by means of vague standards, they will continue to prioritize reluctantly and ineffectively. Everything has some importance to some residents. Regardless of how the organization deals with its inability to prioritize, it fails to control its scope of activity.

In order to break free from the prioritization trap, let us look at how municipal activities can be categorized in accordance with the essential characteristics of government. The following five categories are based on the application of local government resources and powers to protect, regulate, monopolize, engage in commerce, and perform noncommercial activities.

Governmental Legislative and Enforcement—the power to protect. This category subsumes the activities that protect people, their property, and their freedom of action. This includes legislating protective laws (e.g., nuisance laws); enforcing state and local protective criminal and civil laws that protect persons, property, and trade; and mediating civil contracts impartially. The corresponding activities center around local ordinance development, policing, law enforcement, courts, and relationships with other levels of government (regional, state, and federal).

Governmental Regulatory—preemptive control. This category includes the municipality's regulation of local activities. Regulation can take the form of laws that restrict specified actions (e.g., prohibition on gaming) or laws that permit certain actions (e.g., land use regulations, nonexclusive franchises). Examples of regulation include planning and zoning, business license, and local legislation aimed at controlling or restricting specified personal or commercial activities.

Municipal Monopoly—exclusive control over commercial activities. This category consists of exclusive enterprise and utility services. Such services can be provided commercially because they do not require the municipality's legislative or enforcement powers. Fire suppression; ambulance; park operations; waste management; water; sewer; and electricity generation and distribution are examples of such services. A municipality can operate a monopoly service directly, or it can appoint an exclusive franchise holder.

Commercial services—participation in commercial activities without exclusive control. This category covers activities that are commercial in nature but for which the municipality does not restrict other local providers. Often, a municipality offers such services alongside private (for-profit or nonprofit) organizations. Recreation programs, parking, childcare, schools, and libraries are common examples of these services.

Noncommercial activities—participation in nongovernmental, noncommercial activities. This category captures all of the noncommercial activities that do not require local government authority to legislate or regulate. Such activities include social, charitable, and advocacy. For example, local programs aimed at economic development, homelessness, sustainability, and social justice fall into this category.

If a municipality cannot determine the category for a given activity, it should examine that activity. Because many city activities comprise smaller activities, some activities may appear to fall under more than one category. For example, *local ordinances* is too broad an activity to place under one category. Such activities need to be broken down into smaller units. Some local ordinances pertain to the protective defining of rights (e.g., quiet enjoyment of one's leased or owned property) while others are regulatory (e.g., rent control). The process of categorizing activities is not intended to resolve complex legal and technical issues, such as when a restriction on property use is rights-protecting and when it infringes upon the property owner's rights. That is a matter for the local courts.

There may be options in terms of whether a non-commercial activity is viewed as supplanting a commercial or nonprofit activity. For example, some aspects of economic development, such as cooperative marketing, can be commercialized. And library and school services can be provided either commercially or noncommercially. Such distinctions are not critical to the evaluation.

A properly functioning government is an essential element of any flourishing community. When local government does not function well for any reason, the personal and commercial communities cannot function well either. For local government to function well, municipal officials need to understand the activities undertaken by their organizations in terms of what government is and what it is not. The nature of government determines the areas in which it can be efficacious and those in which its legislative and enforcement authority cannot contribute positively to the community. Municipal officials need to ensure that the scope of their organizations is aligned with these facts. These five categories facilitate that alignment.

If one accepts that communities need a legislative authority to define and enforce personal and property rights to ensure residents' and business owners' freedom to engage in personal and commercial activities—a question remains: How should a city government make decisions that fulfill such purposes? I examine that question next.

8

Municipal Decision-Making Understood

I promised a framework for understanding and resolving the municipal financial crisis. So far, I have provided an account of what local government is and described its value to residents and businesses. I have also provided a classification scheme that describes local government activities in terms of their relationship to governmental, commercial, and personal interactions and transactions. Municipal officials then need a clear decision-making standard and a principled decision-making method with which to apply this foundational information to decide the conditions under which it is proper to use local government resources and powers to protect (governmental legislative and enforcement), regulate (governmental regulatory), monopolize (municipal monopoly), engage in commerce (commercial services), or perform noncommercial activities.

I stated earlier that if cities can manage their way into insolvency, they can manage their way out. A new decision-making process, integral to the new framework, is key to how they can manage their way to organizational and financial stability. But first, we need to examine the traditional decision-making approach, including its value-driven standards and methods.

A municipality's failure to control its scope of activity leads to the inability to control its costs, causing it to grapple with unwieldy budget deficits. Invariably, someone new to the scene, a new elected official, a new administrative manager, or a newly engaged resident asks: "How did we get here?" There are three common answers to this question—none of which I found satisfactory.

M. Moses, *The Municipal Financial Crisis*,
https://doi.org/10.1007/978-3-030-87836-8_8

One answer blames meager results on inferior execution. Poor outcomes thus stem from the inadequacies of civic leadership, public engagement, city management, staff, technology, and work methods. If only there were more competence in these areas, the city organization would be more efficacious. The second answer says our expectations are unrealistic. Things do not always work out ideally—or even satisfactorily—nor should anyone expect them to. After all, according to this thinking, this is the government at work. Both perspectives lead to cynical resignation at a time when communities need positive engagement and better thinking.

The most plausible answer—one that sitting councils often embrace—is that their predecessors made bad financial decisions.

Certainly, city councils have made many poor financial decisions. But financial considerations do not drive decision-making. City organizations are not profit-driven in their organizational structure or in their missions: they act to achieve a broader set of objectives related to their residents' quality of life. To understand how we got to where we are today, it is the values approach driving city government decision-making that we need to examine. It is the values approach that determines when and how municipal officials decide to deploy the organization.

Group Force vs. Individual Freedom Decision-Making

When considering whether the local government should engage in an activity, municipal officials need to (but seldom do) recognize that there are two basic types of decision-making processes: one in which collective decisions are implemented by force, and one in which individually autonomous decisions are expressed in voluntary actions. From this, two decision-making models emerge: The *group force model* and the *individual freedom model*. The group force model employs collective decisions that are imposed by force when it is collectively deemed appropriate. It is a decision-making model that does not permit dissent. The individual freedom model prioritizes the autonomy of residents and business owners—preserving competition and choice. It is a decentralized form of decision-making where these agents can make independent judgments about how to achieve their own goals, dealing with each other voluntarily when mutual agreement is possible or going their separate ways when it is not.

Given the nature of their organizations, local governments necessarily make decisions via the group force model. They make decisions where all residents, in principle, have input—and where the outcomes of those decisions are imposed on all residents. Think of the criminal code. Should cannabis production be criminalized in our city? That is not a decision each city resident gets to make independently. It is a decision we all make together, either directly through a ballot proposition or indirectly through our elected representatives. Then that decision is imposed on everyone: if we decide to ban cannabis cultivation, then anyone who tries to grow it will face coercive penalties.

Consistent with their missions and visions, city governments often jump into an activity with a vague sense that the activity is desirable. They do not pause to assess whether this activity is best handled through group force decision-making, or individual freedom decision-making. They ignore two crucial and related questions: (1) Does this activity *require* an agency empowered with the right of force; and (2) What do we *lose* if we use force to impose a decision on all, brooking no dissent? The first question is important because there are some goals that can only be achieved through force, such as protection from criminals—while others can at least potentially be provided by private individuals and groups. The second question helps us identify, in cases where the activity does not require the lawful use of force, any potential negative consequences of using government, whose distinctive power is not the capacity to produce, but the power to legislate. When the authority of the city government is employed, we lose the benefits of the autonomy of producers and consumers. When the city government restricts producers, the advantages of competition and ingenuity are lost, as are the advantages of consumer choice. These losses are glossed over when decision-making is centralized, and the costs are obscured.

The group force model of decision-making is vital to the ability of residents and businesses to flourish—but *only* when it is used for the purpose of *preserving the individual freedom model*. We do need local governments vested with the power to use force. But we need them to protect the ability of individual residents and business owners to act free from force.

For example, there is nothing lost and much gained by leaving individuals free to decide which businesses to start, how much to charge for their products, whom to hire and whom to fire, which hobbies to pursue, which homes to build and where. Using the group force model to govern such decision-making means imposing some people's preferences on others. But individuals cannot make independent decisions about such matters if they are subject to the arbitrary will of murderers, thieves, vandals, and conmen. Thus, the community makes a collective decision to stop and punish violent criminals and fraudsters so residents can make independent decisions about how to live their own lives.

The freedom to act and associate is a fundamental human need. As such, it is a prerequisite to human flourishing at the only level that value pursuit takes place—or that human flourishing can be achieved—i.e., individually. That is not to deny that community is a genuine value. It certainly is. But a community is not something over and above the people who make it up. And residents can enjoy that value only if they can each make independent decisions about how to associate with other community members. For the collection of individual residents in a community to flourish, everyone must be free to exercise his or her own judgment in pursuit of his or her chosen values.

Auberon Herbert made the point in this way:

> There is one and only one principle, on which you can build a true, rightful, enduring and progressive civilization, which can give peace and friendliness and contentment to all differing groups and sects into which we are divided—and that principle is that every man and woman should be held by us all sacredly and religiously to be the one true owner of his or her faculties, of his or her body and mind, and of all property, inherited or—honestly acquired.[1]

Every municipality I worked with strove to figure out how to meet the needs of residents. But they all overlooked residents' fundamental human needs when deciding when and how to use the organization's authority. By not using group force decision-making exclusively to protect individual decision-making, local government compromises the flourishing of its residents.

Decision-Making Standards

If the group force decision-making model is not bound by the need to protect individual decision-making, what then governs municipal decisions? And what would compel municipal officials to set aside financial considerations when making decisions? The answer to both of these questions lies in the traditional decision-making standards.

---

[1] Auberon Herbert, *The Voluntaryist Creed* (Oxford: Oxford University Press, 1908), 68.

Even in the face of insolvency, cities add new programs and services—e.g., sustainability, public wireless networks, homelessness, economic development, business aid, housing, etc. Why does not an indisputably dire financial position protect cities today from more deficit spending, further pushing out obligations to future taxpayers, or a greater dependence on state or federal relief? The answer is: for the same reason that I could not avert most of the scope creep when I was a finance director. The justification for these activities—trumping anyone's concerns about the financial consequences, secondary impacts, and limitations on what the organization can realistically deliver—is that the program or service is in the *community interest* (sometimes expressed as community benefit or public interest). This activates group force, not as a means to protect individual freedom, but as a tool to enact the community interest. The unclear definition of *community interest* constitutes a loophole that exposes the city organization to manipulation, misuse, and financial negligence. If something is determined to be in the community interest, then city governments conclude that group force must be used to achieve it—even in the face of the city's organizational and financial deterioration and regardless of its impact on individual residents and business owners.

The problem is that the *community interest* lacks a clear definition—but not because municipal officials have lazily ignored the question. It lacks a clear definition because, in its popular use, it is a murky concept. Although we can talk about the *community* in the context of the people who reside in the city and the business owners who trade there, the *community* is not a distinct entity possessing interests. Only individuals have interests. Individuals may form groups based on shared or mutual interests, but the group qua group does not have an interest. Similarly, *benefits* are realized at the individual, or private, level. Thus, *community interest* and *community benefit* are neither clear nor reliable standards for decision-making.

One observer makes a similar point about the sister term to community interest—*public interest*: "While it is one of the most used terms in the lexicon of public administration, it is arguably the least defined and least understood – few public officials would have any clear idea what the term actually means and what its ramifications are in practice."[2] This is consistent with what I have seen in city council and municipal board settings. No one in municipal government can explain what they mean by community interest, community benefit, or public interest. Nor does anyone try to define these terms. Yet all of these constitute criteria for placing more and more aspects of

[2] Chris Wheeler, "The Public Interest: We Know It's Important, But Do We Know What It Means," *AIAL Forum* 2, no. 48 (2006): 12.

personal life and commercial activity under the *group force model*. Such intervention comes at the expense of residents' and business owners' autonomy and the municipality's viability.

What are the consequences of applying a standard that is utterly unclear? Who benefits and who suffers when an equivocal standard is accepted and applied?

Because there is no objective way to distinguish between what is in the community interest and what is not, in practice the community interest consists of whatever a majority of a city council or municipal board say it is. This unleashes the ongoing struggle among those who want to use the legislative powers of municipal government to define *community interest*. Virtually every local conflict that I saw consisted of pressure groups arguing that they represent the community and that their interests are the community's interests. Consider city planning and the wrestling over development and land use issues: growth vs. no-growth, big box encouraged vs. big box prohibited, NIMBY vs. YIMBY, large lot subdivisions vs. small lot subdivisions, high density residential housing vs. low density residential housing, restrictive building and zoning codes vs. permissive building and zoning codes, etc.

One product of this decision-making approach is that city organizations routinely facilitate transfers of wealth by expanding or reducing restrictions on property use (via zoning or planning requirements). When the city increases restrictions on property use, the value of developed properties rises—thus benefiting some property owners. But this intervention comes at the expense of the owners of undeveloped property seeking to sell or develop their land. When restrictions are relaxed, undeveloped properties are suddenly more valuable. Rather than being determined by a willing market, property windfalls and devaluations are decided by political favor.

Those who influence the city council can dominate any local issue. The result is ad hoc initiatives that direct city government resources and group force decision-making to pet projects such as property acquisition, rezoning, recreation and sports venues, public art, etc. Local cronyism is not only enabled, it is inevitable. The crony circle includes the labor unions that help elect city councilmembers and affect their tenure. Labor unions' influence on municipal officials ensures that municipal employees are treated as an extension of the community (i.e., stakeholders) when major organizational issues are considered. But bestowing this political status upon employees impairs city officials' ability to make changes to the workforce.

How should city management weigh long-term consequences once city officials declare an action's community benefit? And how should the city organization address residents and business owners who do not benefit—and perhaps suffer—from an action that city officials decide yields a community benefit? Are such questions not answered because no one ever asks them—or because there are no satisfactory answers?

Now, residents, businesses, and city staff are accustomed to the politicization of local issues. It is difficult to imagine an alternative forum for resolving local issues of land use, building standards, utility services, etc. Although complaints about special interests abound, there is little voice for solutions that would move the management of these issues outside the domain of local political factions. To do so would require moving them outside the sphere of the city organization and, therefore, the sphere of those who influence it.

Amid this politicization, it is understandable that the financial consequences of the city's vast actions—all taken in the name of *community interest*—are disregarded, even when those consequences are devastating. A decision-making approach can either support or hamper sound thinking and analysis. If a key criterion is not only undefined, but *undefinable*, the door is open to organizational and financial chaos. City officials have spawned an avoidable financial crisis through their indifference to the consequences of their actions. These city officials justify their actions using inferior decision-making standards that enable and sustain a precarious values framework.

If we want city governments to be liberating and not menacing, we must take seriously that they operate by *group force* decision-making—and that it is reckless and unjust to use group force in the service of an undefined and *undefinable* goal, like the community interest. But that is not what we are taught. We are taught that the community interest is self-evidently the purpose of governments—and that governments are not agents of force, but flexible, formless tools for achieving that interest. For example, let us look at this statement, a "call for values in government in the internet age," expressed by a director at the Harvard Kennedy School of Government:

> We need to figure out collectively what our values are, how they relate to concrete priorities, and how a revamped government could best deliver on those priorities working for the common good instead of special interests.... If we want to continue living in a prosperous, safe, thriving democracy, we need to start talking about the government we need and want and then take steps to make it a reality.[3]

[3] Nicco Mele, quoted in *Transparency: A Means to Improving Citizen Trust in Government* (Chicago: Government Finance Officers Association, 2018), 5, https://gfoa.org/materials/transparency-a-means-to-improving-citizen-trust.

If taken in quickly, this statement may sound positive and aspirational. But a different tone emerges when we read it more closely, keeping in mind that imprecision works against our understanding and that the city government is characterized by its power to compel.

"We need to figure out collectively what our values are." There is no reliable process to determine values in this way. Different people value different things. As individuals living among other individuals, we often have *mutual* values, but that is a different matter that we manage voluntarily.

Continuing, "how they relate to concrete priorities." Whose priorities as interpreted by whom?

Then, "and how a revamped government could best deliver on those priorities." If we learned anything from the Reinventing Government campaign in the 1990s, it is that government does not readily reinvent, transform, or revamp. And how will it deliver? What a city government *delivers* must be produced or funded by the residents and business owners. Under the *individual freedom model*, individual priorities are met through individual producers competing, successfully meeting those priorities, or going out of business.

And, "working for the common good instead of special interests." What prevents the special interests from representing themselves as the common good? The only common good is the good that residents actually have in common—i.e., protecting their individual freedom to associate and make autonomous decisions.

Then, "If we want to continue living in a prosperous, safe, thriving democracy, we need to start talking about the government we need and want." Without specific criteria, soliciting needs and wants invites an ambitious scope that is tied neither to the nature of government nor to the fundamental needs of the residents nor to fiscal stability.

Finally, "and then take steps to make it a reality." Here we must be clear who is taking what steps. The reality of government is the *group force model*. The *steps* a city government takes to make something a reality calls for compulsion. The conditions necessary for residents and businesses to flourish—*that* is the reality to be made. The city government should be a means to that end and not a vague vision that becomes an end in itself.

Perhaps this is why I stopped getting invited to local government brainstorming meetings.

Decision-Making Methods

To understand how the vague standard of community interest shapes municipal decision-making, it is helpful to look deeper at the conditions under which city councils operate. While in theory, a city council could justify *anything* by reference to the community interest, in practice, what it can do is constrained by objections from stakeholders. In a typical city, the least objectionable ideas prevail. Thus, the preferred approach is to make decisions incrementally—in a way that poses the fewest objections to the status quo, i.e., the previously attained consensus.

Incremental decision-making in municipal government is characterized by the preference for non-radical (often, but not always, *small-scale*) decisions. This approach has several reinforcing conveniences. First, staff experience less pressure. They conserve time by not having to gather as much information as would be needed to justify a wholesale or controversial change. Often, there is not enough information available to garner support for a major change, yet city officials believe some action is called for. In such a case, city officials are more comfortable when they agree to moderate actions that they can walk back if necessary. With lower stakes, it is easier for the city council to reach agreement. Finally, the city can implement incremental adjustments more quickly and with fewer management and resource challenges than sweeping changes require.

Whether in the approval of the annual budget, staffing levels, or the municipal code, the focus of incremental decision-making is on what is changing. The annual budgeting process focuses on spending changes in the upcoming year, staffing plans focus on additions to and deletions of authorized staff positions, and municipal code updates focus on the implications of specific language modifications. When decisions are framed this way, the impact seems manageable—particularly when proposed changes are small in relation to the status quo. For example, although the city council may be approving a staffing complement of 405 employees, its attention is on the three positions that the city manager proposes to add.

Unfortunately, this decision-making approach creates the complications that city officials wanted to avoid. Much of the time I spent with cities was directed to compensating for problems that were preventable had staff gathered more information and applied refined, holistic analysis. Measured changes are a gateway to a series of changes whose cumulative impact is often unfavorable. For example, many city initiatives to address homelessness and vice crimes begin as small, temporary, and non-radical—e.g., a limited pilot program. Then, when these programs are ineffective, city officials expand them. Later, the city makes the programs permanent. It does so not due to any particular success but because there is no graceful exit strategy.

The focus on incremental changes comes at the expense of the big picture. Decision-makers are drawn to *what is changing*, thus tacitly endorsing the status quo. But when municipal officials accept the status quo without scrutiny, they entrench it more so. Then, the measured change of this year is embedded in the status quo when the next year comes. It does not necessarily take a full year for a change to root. I have seen city officials approve new programs because they were told that there were sufficient resources available to support these programs. Then, only a brief time later—and before the programs launched—they learned that the funding resources had been overestimated. Rather than withdraw their approval of the new programs, the city officials pushed forward, thus amplifying the financial strain.

It is true that city councils reach consensus more easily when proposed changes are undramatic. But this is of minimal consolation when the succession of incremental changes brings the organization to a brink where only major course changes can preserve financial solvency. City officials have achieved consensus at the expense of a principled decision-making process. They pursued paths that fewer would have supported if more complete information had not been sacrificed to that consensus. Thus the puzzlement of successor leaders who wonder what the previous leadership was thinking.

When the incremental decision-making approach fails to yield satisfactory results, municipal organizations respond defensively. Municipal officials revise the definition of success to mean the preservation of local services as they are. When I see this, I know that the organization is operating in survival mode. When a municipality hunkers down, its managers abandon the opportunity to improve the status quo in favor of their intense effort to preserve it. At some point, the municipal officials notice that the organization's ability to support the residents and local businesses has withered.

Unintended Consequences and Merely Consequences

Under the traditional decision-making approach, group force is wielded for a nebulous end, the community interest, constrained only by incremental decision-making. This decision-making approach often adds up to major changes over time but without the clear-headed intentionality residents need municipalities to engage in. Predictably, the results are often disastrous. To understand municipal decision-making, there is one further question: Why is the predictable routinely ignored?

A city's aggressive pursuit of retail and commercial expansion, motivated by sales tax revenue, impairs housing development. When new housing cannot keep up with demand, home prices rise, negatively affecting their affordability. Meanwhile, the city offers incentives and special concessions to new businesses, hurting existing local businesses by adding competitors before the market conditions justify their entry. Services for homeless inhabitants attract more transients, worsening problems associated with those who live on the streets or in camps. Complex building codes and high fees impel residents to make unpermitted home repairs. Students and low-skilled residents cannot find work because minimum wage laws set the price of their labor above its market value. When questioned about the negative effects of their decisions, municipal officials often label such effects *unintended consequences*.

But is this characterization correct? None of these consequences is shocking, surprising, or even difficult to predict. Then in what sense are the consequences *unintended*? Consider this from Frank de Zwart's discussion of unintended but not unanticipated consequences:

> We cannot explain these outcomes as arising out of error, ignorance, or blindness as with conventional unintended consequences; the question is not why policy makers failed to anticipate these effects but why, given the foreseen risks, they chose to go ahead anyway. It may be that policy makers are opting for the lesser of two evils, thinking that not acting is worse than permitting the harm they foresee. It may be that they are indifferent to future harm, or simply willing to gamble, hoping things will not turn out too badly. But it may also be that the decisions that produced the unintended harm were carefully weighed on a moral scale.[4]

What *moral scale* would trap a city council in an endless series of undesirable consequences? In the case of city government decisions, the moral scale is a political sliding scale: a scale calibrated, not to protecting the autonomy of residents so they are free to pursue their goals, but to *claims of community interest*. When decision-makers are focused on the vague, undefinable standard of community interest, they lose sight of the actual costs and benefits to individual residents—i.e., those who compose the community. The group force model when used to achieve the *community interest* does succeed. It succeeds at that which it was intended to achieve: the subordination of those

[4] Frank de Zwart, "Unintended But Not Unanticipated Consequences," *Theory and Society* 44, no. 3 (December 2015): 283, https://doi.org/10.1007/s11186-015-9247-6.

who are not considered part of the community interest to those who are, for any given decision-making context.

The local issues that these city actions are intended to address are *real*: i.e., housing, business prosperity, homelessness, and worker productivity. But city officials have adopted values that commit them to resolving these issues by forcing one class of residents to subordinate to another. This cannot help but generate undesirable effects that are convenient to dismiss as unintended consequences. But *consequences* are *merely consequences*. A healthy decision-making framework incorporates—and neither ignores nor disavows—foreseeable consequences.

The Path Forward

The municipal financial crisis will not inspire, scare, or shock municipalities into achieving financial stability. The same mission, vision, and goals that prevented them from doing so endure. They endure because the same assumptions, values, and decision-making methods for deploying the organization endure. This dynamic is not limited to organizations in financial turmoil. Even cities that have been through a municipal bankruptcy process that allowed them to substantially reduce debt and other financial obligations are not immune. If city officials do not follow a financial fresh start (to the extent that bankruptcy allows) with a fresh look at the standards they use to justify the organization's involvement, they effectively hit the snooze button.

The municipal financial crisis did not emanate from reckless financial neglect. (Though I can understand why one might think so.) It is the natural consequence of an organization's value-driven goals—goals justified by vague standards and bad assumptions. Without an understanding of what government is and what its value is to residents and businesses, municipalities cannot establish clear standards. Nor do they have a framework for cultivating good assumptions.

The new framework requires municipal officials to challenge mistaken assumptions, acknowledge what local government is, respect residents' individual need for autonomy, curtail vague decision-making standards that enable gratuitous use of group force, and take responsibility for *all* consequences of their decisions. Next, I will apply this framework to municipal budgeting.

9

Budgeting for Scope

Understanding what city government is, what it is capable of doing, and what it is incapable of doing provides a starting point for municipal officials to decide when and how to exercise local authority. A clear standard of purpose—i.e., to protect individual decision-making—addresses the needs of residents and delimits the organization's scope. Such a decision-making standard subordinates the use of group force to the regard for residents' decision-making autonomy. This autonomy enables residents to pursue their individual values in the community. By properly regarding what government is, using a decision-making standard for engaging the organization that is consistent with the residents' individual needs, and considering all effects of the organization's actions—municipalities have a new framework with which to move forward to undertake the proper scope of the organization's activity.

When I watched municipal officials approve new programs on behalf of the organization, their response to doubters was: "If it doesn't work, we can always change it." Municipalities need to make good on this promise. And they should start by changing the decision-making approach that gives rise to the proliferation of its activities and that distances the organization from its residents. As the agent of the local monopoly on force, the truly successful and sustainable municipal organization ensures that it is doing *only* the things that it should be doing.

So, what is my solution to the municipal financial crisis?

M. Moses, *The Municipal Financial Crisis*,
https://doi.org/10.1007/978-3-030-87836-8_9

Budgeting for Scope

A municipality can achieve control operationally and financially by bringing its activities under control. It can realize this aim by conscientiously scoping its activity. The organization's scope of activity encompasses its full range of activities. *Scoping* constitutes an evaluation of these activities based on an appropriate standard. Such evaluations occur whenever municipal officials decide to create, maintain, or change an activity in which the organization engages. (I continue to use *activity* rather than *service* to describe municipal actions generally because many resource-consuming city actions are not services—e.g., local legislation development and enforcement, federal and state advocacy, land use planning, etc.).

Budgeting for Scope is a process by which the municipal organization decides its scope of activity. The scope is based on those activities for which government power (i.e., group force) is needed to protect the freedom and autonomy of residents and business owners (i.e., the purpose of government).

Budgeting for Scope completes the new framework. It integrates the causal relationship between activities and costs; the nature of government (as contrasted with that of commercial and noncommercial organizations); the value of government as established by the fundamental needs of residents and business owners; and elements of decision-making (methods, value-driven standards, and assumptions).

In order to integrate these elements, the Budgeting for Scope solution incorporates the following three pertinent factors that have been neglected and undermined in conventional fixes:

Activities drive costs. The city organization must control its activities to control its costs. The relationship between scope of activity and control over spending is that of *cause and effect*. I saw this when I was in an organization that was desperately shedding people and programs—i.e., the drivers (causes) of its costs (effects). At first, I was disoriented by the financial results that ensued. After years of watching the city's costs spiral upward, they dropped suddenly and dramatically. The major contributor to US cities' ability to weather the COVID-19 storm is that the reduced level of municipal activity in 2020 constrained spending. Costs *are* in the organization's control, but only if the organization controls the causes of those costs.

The city organization consumes resources that must first be produced by residents and businesses. Strictly speaking, governmental activities do not create economic value. City revenues from taxes and mandatory fees derive from economic value produced in private, commercial activity. Without recognizing this fact, one cannot fully evaluate the personal and financial impact of a city's actions on its residents and business owners. Under existing city funding structures and their reliance on local taxes and mandatory fees, cities can benefit their residents and local economies by not taking from them unnecessarily.

Values, benefits, and interests are applicable only to individuals. Only individuals can choose and pursue values and thus have interests. Extending the measures of values, benefits, and interests to the community invites the abuse of group force. The community, an aggregate of individual residents, has one common interest with respect to local government: that group force is used to protect individual freedom and autonomy. For a local government to fulfill this aim, it must regard the most easily marginalized and neglected constituency, the *individual resident*.

Scoping requires subjecting *all* services, programs, and other activities to the following assessment:

> Does this activity require the local government's legislative and enforcement powers to protect residents, businesses, and their property?

Let us look at how a municipality can evaluate its activities and decide its proper scope of activity using the five classification categories developed in Chapter 7. Some activities may straddle two categories until they are broken down into smaller units. Otherwise, most municipal activities should fall clearly into one of the categories.

Governmental Legislative & Enforcement—the power to protect. This category lies at the heart of government and the heart of a government's value to its constituents. The sustained protection of residents and business owners, their property, and their freedom of action cannot be achieved through private action. The protective activities of local government include legislation creation, legislative review, law enforcement, policing, jurisprudence, and coordination with other levels of government (regional, state, and federal). Such activities are found in municipal police departments, the offices of the city attorney and city manager, and in the local courts. These activities should be examined to ensure that they satisfy the standard of protecting the autonomy of residents and businesses.

The focus of legislative authority should be on criminal and civil laws that protect persons, property, association, and trade. Laws in this category should be rights-defining and rights-enforcing (e.g., nuisance laws) rather than regulatory. The components of any part of the organization's legislative and enforcement activity that are not rights-defining and rights-protecting (i.e., do not protect individual decision-making and action) should be separated from the activity and stopped.

Police activities should be evaluated by a similar standard of how they protect the autonomy and actions of individual residents. When evaluating these activities, one cannot assume that because a police department does something, or has done something historically, such activity is protective under this standard.

The scope of activity in this category should be rigorously defined to ensure that it is consistent with the protective charge of the agency. Further, this scope should be actively managed so it stays consistent with such charge over time.

Governmental Regulatory—preemptive control. This category contains activities for which local government authority is exercised to prohibit or regulate certain activities outside the scope of protecting persons, property, and trade. Often, there is a protective rationale for such activities that needs to be examined. If the activity is protective, it should be part of the legislative and enforcement category. Evaluating activities in this category requires that municipalities answer the question: Does this activity, which uses governmental power to restrict action, have a clear basis in rights-protection? Those regulations without a demonstrable basis in rights-protection should be terminated.

For example, a ban on the sale of vaping products to adults restricts the freedom of both a willing seller and a willing buyer. There is no justification for anyone to interfere with the parties to a commercial transaction of this type. On the contrary, the local government should protect the freedom of sellers and buyers to conduct such free trade.

The enforcement of building regulations also limits commerce. A homeowner and contractor need permission to make certain changes to a home. The stated purpose of the building regulations is to ensure a safe structure. But if local government were not performing this activity, certainly insurance companies would have an interest in the quality of improvements to the homes that they insure. Such companies would establish standards that homeowners would need to follow when modifying their property. And, by contract, homeowners would have to follow such standards. Right behind the insurer is the mortgage lender who requires insurance as a condition of its loans. The point here is that even though the legislation and enforcement of building regulations is outside the scope of protective government, to abruptly drop all building regulations would not serve anyone. The parties who have been relying on the municipality's long history of involvement in critical aspects of this activity need time to make their own adjustments.

Other areas of local regulation raise similar issues with respect to their termination. One can argue that a city should, in the short term, maintain its massage ordinance. Even though such regulations restrict voluntary adult behavior, some landlords rely on the terms of local massage ordinances rather than incorporate similar use restrictions in their leases. It is not fair to such landlords to drop a local legal restriction that they relied on when establishing their lease, without a reasonable notice period.

Whenever issues arise with respect to the community's reliance on regulations restricting or permitting actions, the city's goal should be to terminate its coercive regulations in favor of the voluntary sphere in which those with more direct interest (like those insurance companies, mortgage lenders, landlords, and tenants) can work out contractually the terms of activities that do not infringe on the rights of others.

Land use regulation will also require time to reform. To suddenly drop zoning restrictions or abruptly change land entitlement rules without considering all of the effects is a disservice. But to continue the politicization of land use indefinitely stifles the advancement of local property rights. Cities will need to develop specific strategies and timelines to address this area of regulation.

Meanwhile, local business licensing and other regulation of commercial activities are straightforward to phase out. Many people overestimate the assurance provided by city-issued business and other commercial licenses. The only real assurance is that the license holder filed a form and paid a tax. Other certifications and permits are also misleading. Although such government-issued authorizations (e.g., building occupancy or use permits) may be proof of meeting certain requirements at the time of issuance, their value does not extend beyond that. One's ability to determine the reputation of a business or the condition of a building does not require the authority of local government.

Municipal Monopoly—exclusive control over commercial activities. Residents and businesses rely heavily on several commercial services that municipalities have monopolized, such as water, wastewater, electric utilities, transportation, and fire services. Most of the activities performed by municipalities in these areas are outside the proper scope of local government. Municipalities should phase out the commercial elements of these activities and retain only those that protect the community (e.g., impacts on common waterways under the municipality's jurisdiction).

There is a huge opportunity to tap into private sector ingenuity and creativity. Once telecommunications was demonopolized in the mid-1980s, it did not take long for the cost of telephones and phone calls to drop substantially. Then, as internet technology emerged, the competing telecommunications companies contributed innovations at a pace that no monopoly could achieve. Municipalities have a similar opportunity to unleash the creativity and productive power of the private sector. Such municipalities will face more severe problems than they face currently if they wait until a technological disruption—akin to mobile phones, microprocessors, GPS, and Uber—devalues their utility infrastructure and service delivery systems.

Although the changes from commercializing utilities and other enterprises will be dramatic and exciting, they will not be immediate or routine. When a municipal organization has been operating a utility or other local service for decades, it cannot expect to call on a robust pool of prospective private businesses or operators equipped to take over. There is no incentive for anyone to develop or invest in services in which a local government has legislated a monopoly. Establishing or reestablishing a market takes time.

Nor will such changes come without setbacks. Not all private companies are well-managed. Some people worry that a commercial market in the area of water, wastewater, electricity, and other utilities would not be as competitive or vibrant in comparison to the markets of retail, technology, and personal services. But the answer to: How would the market be truly competitive in the area of utilities? will never be found if municipalities continue to use their authority to make the existence of such a market impossible.

In the meantime, these utility and other enterprise activities need to be rigorously defined and delimited so they can be managed effectively during the period of transition.

Commercial services—participation in commercial activities without exclusive control. This category covers activities that are commercial in nature but for which the municipality does not restrict other local providers. Often, a municipality offers such services alongside private (for-profit or nonprofit) organizations. Recreation, childcare, and libraries are common examples of these services. Municipalities should phase out such activities as quickly as possible.

Cities failed their residents when they undertook endeavors for which local government powers are not required. By commandeering these *services* and operating outside the market, city organizations quell competition and innovation. And the creativity and effectiveness of city employees suffer when they operate these programs as a municipal utility. Imagine having to run a recreation or seniors program following cumbersome city purchasing policies, recruiting under city personnel rules, and competing with police, fire, and public works departments for the city council's attention. The COVID-19 response revealed the financial exposure of city organizations in these areas as well as the complications of managing multidisciplinary activities during a crisis.

Fortunately, there is enormous precedent for nonprofit and commercial fulfillment of needs and demands in these areas. Cities have done a disservice to residents by using current and future tax dollars to discourage such private solutions. Cities underestimate and demean the community when they operate on the premise that residents and businesses will forever fail to find a way to provide recreational or senior programs. Similar activities flourish, such as bowling, chess clubs, bingo nights, lacrosse, little league baseball, Pop Warner football, and martial arts. A decline in the popularity of these activities is not a risk factor for city governments. Nor are expansions, innovations, or changes in the delivery of services in these areas political issues. Contrast the decision-making efficiency of the private sector with that of the city when confronted with whether to offer a recreational or competitive sports program, what size swimming pool to build, which age groups to accommodate in a childcare program, etc.

Noncommercial activities—participation in nongovernmental, noncommercial activities. Noncommercial activities that neither require local government powers nor deliver vital services upon which residents and businesses depend should be the easiest to stop. These activities should be evaluated to determine whether they have any basis in protecting residents from demonstrable physical harm. Those activities without such a basis should be terminated as soon as possible.

These special programs invariably suffer from two factors that haunt local government and add financial burden. The first is municipal officials' tolerance of ambiguous definitions and indeterminate scope. For example, as with *community interest* and *financial sustainability*, no one offers a clear explanation of *sustainability* or *social justice*. But a city cannot budget effectively for a nebulous activity. City officials and budget simulator operators already struggle to weigh the spending of $100,000 on police protection, roof repair, and recreation programs. Without invoking *community interest*, how do city officials establish the merits of $100,000 spent on any activity that no one can define satisfactorily?

The second factor, which extends from the first, is a municipality's failure to show why such initiatives require the use of group force—i.e., why they should even be undertaken by the city organization. When a city takes on initiatives that are neither clear nor clearly addressing threats to residents, the door is open to manipulation, abuse, and taxpayer risk. Time and again, these poorly conceived interventions backfire: minimum wage laws that increase local unemployment; plastic product bans that need to be suspended during a pandemic; homeless initiatives that attract more homeless; and, in some states, solar energy and electric vehicle subsidies that steer residents to more expensive and less reliable energy and transportation.

There is a tendency for city officials to underestimate the resources that the organization consumes on activities that appear to be benevolent and of incidental cost (e.g., sponsorship of community events, legislative advocacy in areas of questionable relevance to the city, cultural exchange, etc.). Still, activities drive costs, and the activities that the city retains will drive its future costs. Shedding all activities that do not contribute to its protective role is precisely how the city organization can control spending and lessen the costs endured by the residents and businesses that fund those activities.

These five categories are the cornerstones of the scoping analysis. Budgeting for Scope will help municipal officials decide which activities should continue in the short, medium, and long term—using a clear standard for how and when to deploy local government authority. This is the *only* way city organizations can break from the paradigm of financial scarcity and limit the burden that they impose on residents and businesses. It is also the only way that city organizations can direct operational improvements to those activities that require the use of the organization's powers.

Budgeting for Scope is distinguished from Zero-Base Budgeting and Performance Budgeting because it precedes the budgeting process. The fate of a city's financial course is set in advance of its budgeting process. Therefore, city officials must take control of the factors that set the terms of budget development.

When a municipal organization coercively removes an activity from the voluntary sphere—where mutual exchanges of value prevail—it ensures that some residents benefit at the expense of those with differing goals and priorities. Notwithstanding narrow benefits enjoyed by those whose preferences dominate, I question whether it is in *any* resident's actual interest to live in a community where that which could be accomplished through voluntary means is commandeered by those politically situated. When winners and losers supplant winners and winners, all honest residents lose.

The seen: Cities deliver an enormous volume of recreation programs, senior programs, meals, golf course access, summer camps, etc. to members of the community. In addition, municipalities have delivered stable utility and enterprise services such as water, wastewater, and parking for decades. The unseen: the injustice of benefits lost (i.e., forgone investments, saving, or spending) by residents whose tax dollars and fees were used for the procurement of facilities and operational subsidies required by these activities. The further unseen: the municipal subsidies not funded in real time—i.e., passed on to future taxpayers and ratepayers in the forms of deferred maintenance on utility infrastructure (e.g., parking lots, community centers, recreation facilities, and senior centers) and unfunded employee retirement benefits. The contradiction: The financial support of residents and businesses must be compelled and utilities must be monopolized in order to meet the commercial and recreational needs of the community. The reality: We are indulging in a regrettable deception if we insist that the municipal organizations are the only means to the successful delivery of these services.

A city organization's efforts to end an activity or to transfer or otherwise leave it to commercial or nonprofit enterprises are often derailed by one of two considerations. First, city officials are concerned that once they shed a city activity or service, it is then difficult, and sometimes costly, to bring it back should there be a reason to do so. Second, many city officials are reluctant to withdraw from an activity that helps some residents when the cost is minor in relation to the city's budget or budget deficit. It should not come as a surprise that both considerations are born from the decision-making approach that created and sustains the current crisis.

The heroic city leadership will be those who discover how city government can operate as a government and not as a quasi-business that uses the power of government to prevent business, not as a means to the ends of some residents at the expense of others, and not as an end in itself.

Activities That Are Worth Retaining Are Worth Fixing

Let us turn to the organization's activities that still must be managed, whether because they are an integral part of local government or because they require a transitional period to phase out. It is important that what the organization does, it does well so long as it does it. To achieve this aim, a municipality should commit *short-term* to delineating each continuing activity's purpose and scope, *mid-term* to revamping the service-delivery system under which the activity operates, and *long-term* to managing both of these commitments. Such an orientation is key to the effective management of the organization's scope of activity. Managing the organization's scope of activity is an ongoing process.

The municipal culture's tolerance of—or preference for—vague missions, visions, and goals is exhibited at the level of the organization's departments. When city departments develop their own missions, they usually do not get past the level of generic catchphrases (e.g., economic vibrancy, safe community, quality of life, etc.). In the same way that the criterion for a new city activity is that it have a loose connection to a city-wide goal, the only clear constraint on the scope of a police or fire department is an activity's loose tie to *public safety*. Ambiguous department missions, encouraged by the organization's drive to maximize services, make the management of the scope of activity at the department level seem impossible. This is why city departments always believe that their resources are insufficient to accomplish their respective missions and goals.

Without clearly defined scopes for the police and fire departments, the only way a city council can ensure the physical safety of the residents is to blindly fund these two departments. But city officials have a greater problem than funding a nebulous scope of public safety activities. Vague departmental scopes are supported by the service delivery system underlying the respective department budgets. When city officials approve a city department's budget, they not only approve what the department is doing, they approve the way that it does it. Without a clearly defined scope, there is no way to optimize the service delivery model for operational and cost effectiveness and not for the preservation of traditions or some other end.

For many years, almost no one challenged the scope, funding, or methods of police departments. Behind the shield of *public safety*, traditional staffing arrangements in police and fire departments survive economic slowdowns, recessions, and even bankruptcy. When municipal officials accept public safety activities as fixed bundled packages included under a wide-ranging scope, they propagate the largest contributor to avoidable municipal financial costs that I have encountered.

When police and fire departments must reduce costs, they leave their service delivery structure intact (i.e., number of sworn personnel, use of personnel, work schedules, etc.) and look for other areas to cut. Regardless of long-term impacts, these departments first shed less costly civilian personnel, defer vehicle and equipment funding, and reduce select activities (e.g., enforcement of parking, traffic, and local ordinances; fire inspections; etc.). The primary focus of these departments is on the preservation of sworn police officer and firefighter positions. According to a report sponsored by the Harvard Kennedy School and National Institute of Justice: "'Uniforms have become political currency,' say some [police] chiefs, and replacing sworn staff with civilian employees, say some mayors, has proved politically 'impossible,' even amidst extreme fiscal crises."[1]

---

[1] George Gascón and Todd Foglesong, "Making Policing More Affordable: Managing Costs and Measuring Value in Policing" (Program in Criminal Justice Policy and Management, Harvard Kennedy School, December 2010), https://hks.harvard.edu/sites/default/files/centers/wiener/programs/pcj/files/NewPerspectivesPolicing-MakingPolicingMoreAffordable-Dec2010.pdf, 16.

It is beyond my expertise to lay out a detailed plan for a refreshed mission and new operating methods for a police department. Knowledgeable professionals have been grappling with this issue for decades and have produced valuable guidance. However, if this wisdom is to inform local decisions, city leaders must overcome traditions, special interests, and provincialism. For decades, the police department has avoided scrutiny *because* it is such a critical function. Municipalities need to address this lapse when they implement the new scoping framework. It is difficult to imagine something of greater importance to the residents and businesses that rely upon an efficacious police department. As one police chief reflected on how a growing number of calls for police were unrelated to rights-violating crimes: "We need to reexamine police processes to determine just what requires the armed authority of the state in your living room."[2]

In that same spirit: Is the armed authority of the state required to protect life and property from fires? Is it required to deliver ambulance services? What do residents gain and lose when a city sustains a local monopoly on these services? If volunteer firefighters had less political influence in the 1800s, it is possible that insurance companies might be running firefighting operations and cities would not have expanded into ambulance services. Until recently, one might be concerned that such a private model would increase fire and medical insurance rates. But for more than a decade, fire departments have been billing insurance companies and individuals for the costs of emergency response to vehicle accidents and, under certain conditions, structural fires.[3] The pressure on fire departments to charge for services formerly paid by taxes continues to mount.

In response to the current crisis, some cities may hand over firefighting or ambulance services to another municipality or to a private firm. For the many organizations without such immediate options, it is essential that they carefully manage these activities. I have watched financially challenged cities scramble to find savings at the level of a few thousand dollars; meanwhile, these same organizations endure hundreds of thousands of dollars of expenditures embedded in the unchallenged operational procedures of their fire departments.

[2] George Gascón and Todd Foglesong, "Making Policing More Affordable: Managing Costs and Measuring Value in Policing" (Program in Criminal Justice Policy and Management, Harvard Kennedy School, December 2010), https://hks.harvard.edu/sites/default/files/centers/wiener/programs/pcj/files/NewPerspectivesPolicing-MakingPolicingMoreAffordable-Dec2010.pdf, 5.

[3] Sarah Netter, "Fire Departments Charge for Service, Asking Accident Victims to Pay Up," ABC News, February 3, 2010, accessed June 10, 2021, https://abcnews.go.com/Business/fire-department-bills-basic-services-horrify-residents-insurance/story?id=9736696.

As with the management of police, I defer to operational experts for the analysis of specific staffing impacts on the performance of a fire department. However, I do know that when staffing traditions are sacrosanct, *any* emergency response department loses the ability to organize around emergency response times cost effectively. Firefighters perform a vital service, albeit at an exaggerated cost. For example, traditional fire department deployment calls for assigning the same number of staff to fire engines and fire stations throughout the day, every day—regardless of changing traffic patterns and fire conditions. Thus, fire departments are staffed for peak demand even in periods of low demand. If city leadership and residents value something greater than the continuation of customary practices that come at a huge premium, this area is ripe for a comprehensive revamp.

A city council's decision to continue *any* activity for a specified or unspecified timeframe marks the beginning, not the end, of its decision. Control over the remaining city activities requires that city officials manage all the major components of those activities. For activities that are heavily personnel-driven, this means management control over the workforce. Prior to the turn of the century, a city management employee could spend an entire career without encountering anything other than reliable economic growth periodically interrupted by a mild recession. In such an environment, the noticeable consequences of managing personnel costs loosely were minor. The major economic downturns of this century have exposed the financial vulnerability of cities. Unfortunately, civil service rules (where applicable) and labor contracts are poison pills that preempt the changes necessary to bring cities under financial control.

For example, the fire unions with which I am familiar will not agree to negotiate significant changes to work schedules. In such cases, there is no opportunity for the fire department to transition from 24-hour firefighter shifts to shorter shifts that do not require extensive sleeping quarters and living spaces at fire stations. This is unfortunate because the cost of building and maintaining firefighter housing in the 2020s far exceeds that of such facilities when they were constructed decades ago. Among the negative impacts of such scheduling inflexibility, it is now complex and costly for municipalities to employ female firefighters.

Meanwhile, labor contracts reinforce traditional personnel deployment by codifying the inflexible scheduling schemes. Even if a fire chief sees an opportunity to reduce costs by adjusting the number of firefighting staff scheduled for a given shift, he or she cannot take action until municipal management successfully negotiates with labor representatives. Rigid staffing requirements subject municipalities to employee overtime costs simply to maintain normal operations. Such costs are incurred to ensure contractually required minimum staffing whenever there is a sickness, injury, vacation, or position vacancy (again, regardless of time of day or fire conditions).

Other city labor contracts are no better at supporting the organization's financial resilience. Even when retirement benefits are reduced in bankruptcy or pre-bankruptcy negotiations, the operational *working conditions* provisions of labor contracts are left intact. If an organization that relies so heavily on people to perform its function does not control its personnel and operational work processes, it cannot respond promptly or comprehensively to improve financial results.

Properly executed, work process and technology improvements can be real solutions. But this is possible only when cities apply these strategies to activities whose scopes are well-defined and delimited and that are supported by a workforce responsive to management direction. A few decades ago, it seemed that an organization operating outside the marketplace—i.e., a governmental agency—could afford to operate in an unfocused and inefficient manner. Since that time, the costs and consequences of managing ill-defined activities in a loose manner have become glaringly evident.

Not everyone will agree on which activities are appropriate to terminate first or on exactly how they should be phased out. But the organization should be able to commit to a serious review of service delivery for any activity that continues for as long as that activity continues. Table 9.1 illustrates how a city might manage its timeline for implementing Budgeting for Scope.

Decisions regarding what to phase out and when to phase it out are serious ones. Municipalities—and their residents—live with their council and board decisions for a long time. If I were a municipal official attempting to address the operational and financial stability of the organization, I would want clear principles to evaluate which municipal activities were holding back community members and businesses. I would also want to know which municipal activities were most critical to the residents and businesses, so those areas could be perfected. Without such a perspective, a city official cannot properly direct the organization's resources.

Scoping the Organization's Internal Policies

So far, I have been focusing on the organization's scoping and management of activities that are directed to the community, such as local legislation,

Table 9.1 Actions to support budgeting for scope and service delivery overhaul

Activity	Phase One (immediate / short-term)	Phase Two (medium-term)	Phase Three (long-term and ongoing)
police enforcement (protect)	define scope/overhaul resource deployment and service delivery	implement new deployment	actively manage deployment and service delivery
fire suppression (commercial)	define scope/overhaul resource deployment and service delivery	implement new deployment / evaluate commercial alternatives	(dependent upon results from prior step)
ambulance (commercial)	develop exit strategy	implement exit strategy	
assets not used in provision of core services (commercial)	develop divestiture strategy	sell assets	
unenforced legislation (regulatory)	rescind		
non-protective regulations (regulatory)	prepare phaseout plan	execute phaseout plan	
recreation, childcare, library, golf courses (commercial/noncommercial)	develop exit strategy/discontinue activities where possible	implement exit strategy	
garbage/solid waste (commercial)	develop exit strategy	implement exit strategy	
water, wastewater, other utility (predominantly commercial)	define scope/overhaul resource deployment and service delivery	develop exit strategy/retain protective elements	implement exit strategy/manage protective elements
Economic development (noncommercial)	discontinue activity		

policing, recreation, community events, etc. But there is another dimension to the scope of municipal activity that has financial implications. *How* municipalities conduct their business is an important resource consideration. As municipalities have expanded their role in advocacy (e.g., sustainability, local business promotion, equity and social justice, etc.), they have established formal policies that support such programs. In considering the proper scope of a city organization, it is important to evaluate these programs in terms of their protective value to residents and their effect on the organization's financial stability.

Cities claim to value fiscal prudence. But what does—or can—this mean in the context of spending tax dollars? To some depression-age municipal workers, it meant limiting spending on supplies by hammering used construction nails until they were straight enough to be reused. Today, fiscal prudence is subordinated to other objectives, such as being *green* (a component of broader *sustainability* initiatives) or local economic development. These objectives manifest in *green purchasing* and *local vendor preference* policies. The former policies elevate claims of green (i.e., no or low environmental impact) above economic considerations. The latter policies bestow favorable treatment on a local supplier who competes for a municipal purchase contract.

Which taxpayer's perspective should these purchasing policies consider when introducing such buying criteria? The taxpayer who would pay a premium—for whatever reason—to support anything labeled green or offered locally? The taxpayer who is barely scraping by financially and needs to find the best low-cost alternative when making any kind of purchase? The taxpayer whose economic evaluation of energy tradeoffs differs from that of the city, and who is disturbed by the fact that city spending is sufficiently substantial to be a consideration for any local businesses?

The consequence of green and local purchasing policies is that city organizations pay premium prices for vehicles, buildings, solar panels, electricity, supplies, and more. Such a result is inevitable once the city introduces criteria that supersede operational and cost considerations. In the case of green purchasing policies, the justification for this override is that there are environmental benefits. But *environmental benefit* as a decision-making standard is more nebulous—and further removed from residents—than *community benefit*. Or, put another way, *community* is now expanded to include all of nature—with its animals, plants, rivers, and coastlines.

For a community to flourish, environmental quality is important insofar as it affects the health and well-being of residents. But if the city deploys its powers—not to keep the environment safe and healthy—but to enforce minimal environmental impact as an end in itself, the flourishing of residents is no longer weighed. When *environmental benefit* takes on a life of its own in this way, cities create a hair trigger for the use of group force and aberrant spending. For example, environmental impact reports provide cover for the denial of housing development proposals and commercial and industrial siting applications without proving demonstrable harm to residents. One urban economist points out the incompleteness of environmental reviews: "Each review only evaluates the impact of the project if it's approved, not the impact if it's denied and construction begins somewhere else."[4] I would add the observation that the criteria used in such reviews have evolved from the consideration of the environmental impact on residents to the prioritization of nonimpact to the environment at the expense of residents.

Today, city spending decisions that were once driven by operational requirements and functional specifications are now impelled by detached environmental considerations. I have seen new city facility construction projects emphasize not how to get the most value from the dollars spent, but rather how to obtain the highest environmental certification. Meanwhile, the financial payback period on electric vehicles still exceeds the useful life of these vehicles. Yet, an increasing number of cities are committing to such purchases. Similar cost-desensitized decisions multiplied across city spending amass mammoth opportunity costs and sidestep financial accountability under the cover of city policy.

At the same time, local vendor preferences cost cities as much as ten percent more than they would otherwise pay on qualifying purchases. The justification is that such a policy supports local businesses, particularly those based in high-cost locations. Although part of the cost of the preference may be offset by the sales tax that the city receives on the taxable portion of the procurement, the city absorbs most of the cost of the financial concessions.

When a city organization spends more for something than it needs to, its residents bear the added costs. Some city officials suggest that the premium costs of green and local purchases are necessary so the city can set a good example. Under this view, if the city promotes the limitation of environmental impact and buying local, it should act accordingly.

But why is the city promoting these issues? Again, limiting environmental impact as an independent goal (i.e., without regard for the effect on residents and businesses) does not serve the residents and business owners. And although *buy locally* sounds community friendly, cities do not consider all of the implications of such a policy. We do not suggest that businesses only *sell*

[4] Edward L. Glaeser, *Triumph of the City: How Our Greatest Invention Makes us Richer, Smarter, Greener, Healthier, and Happier* (New York: Penguin Books, 2012), 212.

locally. To do so would seriously debilitate many of them. But if all residents and businesses seriously followed the *buy locally* stance that their respective cities modeled, those residents and businesses would suffer directly in proportion to the value they gave up by making less worthwhile local purchases. In addition, the local businesses would suffer from their loss of trade outside the city.

And there is the deeper question: Is it even proper for a city to *set a good example*? Every resident and business is faced with unique, complex, and dynamic tradeoffs when deciding which light bulbs or vehicles to purchase, where to purchase them, and how to design their homes and buildings. What is accomplished by a city that enacts a model for others to follow? When I had a role in municipal procurement, I found it awkward that we at the city were the only ones watching the example that we were setting. Aside from the green marketers and a few entitled local businesses, no one was paying attention to these purchases.

Nor was anyone paying attention to the financial analysis. When a return-on-investment calculation was needed to demonstrate fiscal sensitivity, the city took the calculations provided by the green vendors at face value. And in retrospect, the sense of entitlement on the part of local businesses is understandable. The city organization created many of the policies that contributed to the inflated cost of doing business locally.

City organizations will not control their spending so long as they sanction ill-conceived programs that subordinate cost considerations without regard to the residents who pay for such programs. There is something amiss when a city's vision to become world class leads to pretentiousness and provincialism. Fortunately, the city organization has only its loosely defined programs and premium costs to lose.

When It Is Too Late

One day, municipal bankruptcy or a state takeover becomes inevitable for some cities. As discouraging and demoralizing as this is, the leadership focus should be on that which is under its control. Some city officials may be tempted to wait and rely on the bankruptcy court or state to sort things out, particularly when the organization's morale is not high. But there is a heavy cost to allowing the run-up to bankruptcy to be a lost year—a year that the city organization could have used to scope activities and focus on its future. Likewise, a state takeover is not a streamlined process.

The bankruptcy court will not dictate the scope of the city organization's activity. Nor will it resolve antiquated service delivery traditions and practices. Nor will the court change the city organization's culture. Only the city leadership can have a purposeful and lasting impact in these areas. Similarly, unless a state manager overrides the city leadership, there is still important work that the organization can take on.

Where the court or state's aid is needed in easing contractual constraints on personnel deployment or compensation, it can do so only if such concerns are clearly identified. Municipal bankruptcy is a painful, expensive process. Much of the organization's financial and analytical capacity is devoted to the bankruptcy, thus detracting from a long-term, operational focus. An impending bankruptcy or state takeover may not seem like an ideal time to address issues such as what the organization should be doing, or how it should perform the activities to which it is dedicated long-term. But these issues will not become easier to resolve later.

A Solution or Just Another Nonsolution

Anticipating a councilmember's cautious question: If Budgeting for Scope is such a promising idea, why haven't we—or why hasn't someone—already done it?

No one has done it because under the traditional decision-making approach, there is no deep-seated scoping problem for cities to solve. No one has done it because no one has been amenable to forgoing a mission to maximize local services and rethinking vague organizational goals rationalized by nebulous standards. No one has done it because no one has asked or answered: "What is a city government?" No one has done it because no one has offered a framework for understanding the municipal financial crisis in fundamental terms. Thus, cities and other municipalities continue to bog down, making minor tweaks to tired and inadequate fiscal sustainability plans.

What distinguishes the Budgeting for Scope and comprehensive overhaul of service delivery described in this chapter from the conventional solutions that I characterized as *nonsolutions*?

Nothing, if city organizations implement these solutions mechanically or as a process from which they expect positive results simply *because* they dutifully follow a set of instructions. Cities have made and reinforced poor decisions because city officials focused on process and not on the full context of their actions. Municipalities prioritize process over results by relying on quorums, voting majorities, public notices, public hearings, public outreach, community surveys, and public comment. While these processes provide political cover for the consequences of municipal decisions, they do not provide cover from the *actual* consequences of those decisions.

Then what principle should city officials follow in the Budgeting for Scope approach? In this case, I recommend heeding William Lloyd Garrison: "Gradualism in theory is perpetuity in practice."

The Budgeting for Scope framework must not be just another *tool in the toolbox*. It is not a solution for cities to use intermittently while keeping a foot in the world of local service maximization and gratuitous use of group force. A municipality that dabbles with the framework or one that regresses to an incremental decision-making approach will not achieve the enduring results needed to relieve its financial turmoil. This framework must *govern* the toolbox. Anything less comes at the continued expense of residents and business owners who deserve better from their local government organizations.

Activities will always drive costs; government will always administer group force; local government will always be funded by the productive efforts of residents and businesses; and individual residents will always be the only ones who can pursue values, enjoy benefits, and have interests. Municipalities that successfully align their scope of activity with these facts will regain control of their spending, their budgeting, and their organizations. Although such municipalities may not fully control their destiny, they will have a framework with which they can begin to shape it.

10

Municipal Government After the Crisis

In the course of taking control of their activities and their organizations, municipalities will discover that they can be effective in supporting the flourishing of residents and thriving of local businesses. Local governments administer group force—and that is a good thing when it is used to protect residents' autonomy and voluntary association. A vague decision-making standard for deploying local government powers leads to unmanageable costs for the organization and terrible results for residents—and that should motivate municipal officials to adopt a clear standard that delimits the organization's activities and promises better results for residents. And the future itself will be improved when it is not ignored—i.e., when municipalities attend to that which they should foresee. A proper framework is indispensable to transcending the confusion rampant in municipal administration, finance, and budgeting.

I have not included mission and vision statements as part of Budgeting for Scope because such statements are a secondary consideration to that solution. Revising a mission and vision without first overhauling the decision-making and values approach that gave rise to it does not fix anything. For completeness, I offer the following model statements:

Mission: Protect the freedom of residents and business owners, minimizing conflicts by defining and protecting property rights.

Vision: Provide the local socio-political conditions for residents to flourish and businesses to thrive.

M. Moses, *The Municipal Financial Crisis*,
https://doi.org/10.1007/978-3-030-87836-8_10

If these statements do not excite us as much as: *Be the best city in the Milky Way Galaxy*, then we need to reflect upon what excites us and why—and whether we are preparing to compound past failures or to redress for success.

The goals that follow from this mission and vision should be specific, measurable, and achievable. Although such guidance seems trite, it should not be taken for granted. City organizations are accustomed to fanciful visions that beget fanciful goals. The countless unsuccessful attempts to incorporate meaningful performance measures into municipal government have left city officials desensitized to the importance of such measures.

In retrospect, the performance measures had to fail. Such measures were often patterned after those developed in commercial environments. Local government needs performance measures based upon its fundamentally different mission. The standard of success for a city is not found in metrics that focus on organizational outputs. It is found in the degree of freedom its residents and businesses enjoy.

Residents, chambers of commerce, and local journalists should ask local municipal officials *why* their organizations are involved in the various activities they sustain. A municipal activity that cannot be shown to protect or preserve the freedom of residents and business owners should be regarded with suspicion. Municipal officials should dispose of—and not recycle—those activities that do not protect individual decision-making. This is how everyone with a stake in local government can ensure that their respective organizations liberate, and not hold back, their communities.

Additional Recommendations, Blind Spots, and Deal Making

Is there anything else that you would recommend?

This is the question that municipal managers would pose to me after I spent an hour presenting my suggested improvements to the organization's administrative and finance systems and policies. At first, I thought that this question was simply a courtesy—extended just to confirm that I had finished making my recommendations. But when the question was repeated, I wondered whether these managers were expecting something more—or something *different*.

I have the same thoughts about how some municipal officials may respond to my recommendations here. City officials associate auspicious proposals with opportunities for awards, press releases, and outsized pairs of scissors for ribbon-cutting ceremonies. When a proposed solution takes on long-standing assumptions and conventions, it necessarily defies prevailing sensibilities. But neither municipal managers nor their councils and boards will solve their problems if they limit themselves to only those courses of action that look the way they expect them to look. Sometimes what is needed is a new framework.

So yes, there is something else that I would recommend. I recommend that municipalities take whatever immediate steps they can to use the new framework to understand their current situation and to scope their way forward.

Implementing changes to the scope of municipal government is going to be difficult for many of the people whose knowledge and experience can contribute to a brighter future. Those most familiar with local government are also those most acclimated to the customs and culture of municipal organizations. After a few years in each of the municipalities I worked, I developed my own blind spots. I lost my ability to see clearly how to conserve the city's resources, whether through improvements to administrative systems or—in my bolder moments—challenges to the organization's scope of activity.

When one sees an opportunity for improvement, they open a window. If the person does not, or cannot, take advantage of that window, it becomes difficult later to recreate or even recognize the same opportunity. Sometimes managers make a deliberate choice to choose their battles: An employee with a poor attitude is the shop steward for the union, rendering disciplinary actions difficult and protracted. An employee with limited ability to adapt to new technology is going to retire soon, so the supervisor and manager do not address his shortcomings. Only the finance department recognizes the need to overhaul a computer system, so no one initiates the change. Invariably, these missed opportunities accumulate to the point that one cannot see them when there is a chance to address them. Not because the system beats you down, an explanation that does little to explain. But because one simply cannot manage in an effective flow if too many unaddressed issues amass.

New managers in my department would sometimes present me with suggested improvements that I had considered just a few years earlier. Often, these were ideas that I abandoned because I chose to focus on other changes. But at some point, I stopped seeing these ideas as opportunities. I became desensitized to and tolerant of conditions that I previously found untenable. Although many in the organization still perceived me as an agent of change, my ability to stay on top of the most needed changes had diminished.

Municipalities need to be aware that these blind spots exist. And municipal leaders need to create a new management flow and a new organizational flow.

The new organizational flow will require a different type of work and skill. In three decades of work in and around municipal government, I can count on one hand the number of local officials that were accomplished dealmakers. By *dealmaker*, I do not mean someone who uses the city's authority to badger a developer into submission by withholding rights of land use. Nor do I mean the creation of a public–private partnership that simply allows a private firm to transfer risk to taxpayers. Nor do I mean someone who declares victory by securing a multiyear labor contract at the cost of the organization's management control and financial stability. I mean someone who has the creativity, vision, and skill to consummate a complex, win-win arrangement with proper regard for the nature of government and respect for residents.

Municipalities do not need entrepreneurs to take over and run local government *as a business*. Such an approach has not worked—and cannot work—at any level of government. Local government is still defined—and confined—by its unique powers. Municipalities need smart and talented people who can decide and implement the organization's scope *as a government*. And their residents and businesses need a government that upholds the freedom of businesses to conduct the activities that should be run *as a business* and the freedom of nonprofits to conduct the activities that should be run as private value pursuits. The demands of rescoping and reconfiguring a city organization or phasing out a municipal service are daunting. Residents will need the best from those municipal managers who are capable dealmakers but who have been trapped in the traditional mission, vision, and decision-making approach.

Most of the problems that current city leaders face have been handed down. Cleaning up other people's messes—playing their foul balls—is often dispiriting and unglamorous. Much of the early progress is thankless and unseen. But the current crisis calls for municipal leadership that can thrive in such an environment. Municipalities need leadership that can make deals its successors and residents will appreciate.

Predictions

What is to become of our cities?

In cities and other municipalities that successfully organize around activities for which their authority is needed to protect their residents, shed monopolistic control of services that preempt competitive solutions, and withdraw from commercial and nonprofit activities that crowd out private organizations—the residents and local economy will flourish. Such cities will see dramatic innovations in areas that the city organization has prevented or discouraged outside participation. I expect to see creative solutions to the delivery of utility services, recreation programs, charitable endeavors, and more. With residents and businesses genuinely engaged in these areas, the upper bounds of what is possible ascend dramatically. In addition to releasing the creativity and synergies lying dormant in their communities, these cities will check cronyism, regain the confidence of their residents, improve their own internal morale, and take control over their financial future. I look forward to the success stories that emerge from this courageous approach.

The success of these exceptional cities will be determined by how well they manage transitional issues. Some cities will struggle to sustain the commitment to managing their scope. Unexpected revenues, an economic upswing, or savings derived from the disciplined management of the city organization's scope of activity can dilute the sense of urgency. A change in elected officials can also disrupt an organization's new vision. Some inside and outside the organization will pressure the city council to delay or cancel the termination of certain programs. Some will push to add new programs.

The response of city officials to such pressures will distinguish the city organizations devoted to a vision of doing the right things well from those dedicated to the traditional model. Another test of these city officials' fortitude is whether proceeds from the sales of city assets are used to benefit those taxpaying and rate-paying residents who paid for those assets, to bail out the organization, or to finance a new city endeavor.

Most importantly, cities that take seriously the value of government to their residents and businesses will deliver that value. These residents will live fully. They will enjoy the autonomy of adults free to plan their days, weeks, and months—adults free to live their lives and pursue their goals. Imagine a community of such residents and what they could accomplish. Success would not be guaranteed, but its prerequisite, freedom, would be ensured by local government. Likewise, commerce thrives when it is protected from forces that disrupt its ability to plan, produce, trade, and enjoy the rewards of success.

Cities that double down on the traditional decision-making model—maximizing municipal services, using vague standards for the exercise of the city's authority, and preventing private and nonprofit sector solutions—will continue to operate in fiscal crisis. The standard of *community interest* establishes a low threshold for the addition of programs, services, and other activities. Meanwhile, it doubles as a high threshold for the discontinuation of activities, whether those activities benefit a vocal few, a hypothetical few, or an assumed many. One cannot suggest that the city organization is going to maximize services guided by the undefinable standard of *community interest* which it will interpret as it goes because it will know it when it sees it—and then, after amassing hundreds of diverse activities that become financially and administratively overwhelming, expect to achieve anything other than a permanent financial crisis.

Some cities may appear to be successful when one focuses only on the seen. For a city, failure is not obvious existentially—at least not in the beginning. And success is not proven merely by a city's ability to fend off insolvency. Most broken cities will avoid bankruptcy, state takeover, and disincorporation. What matters is the extent to which residents and business owners flourish. A city can fail its residents even while continuing to pay its bills.

A failed city suffers in mediocrity, hopeless scarcity, and local cronyism. Yes, such a city can camouflage its failure by mortgaging the future to construct a new building or to preserve its most dilapidated one—until it cannot. Or the city can conceal its service deterioration by shifting attention to the most noticeable activities at the expense of the neglect of those that it can put off—until it cannot. There is always a way to defer decisions until there are no more options—no more decisions to be made. And if a city's leadership accepts such cover-ups as solutions, it becomes the irresponsible regime that burdens the next city leadership and the next generation of residents. A failed city refuses to see and consider the unseen because that is where evidence of failure lies in the present and where it will appear in the future.

Most city organizations are sufficiently provincial that they see themselves as different from other cities but amply insecure that they constantly watch what other cities are doing. Thus, they alternate between rationalizing actions whose justification is vague reference to the city's *uniqueness* and actions whose justification is vague reference to the activities of the herd. The former is used to overcome questions of financial risk in areas for which there are scant examples of success (e.g., sports, entertainment, and convention facilities), while the latter is used to provide cover for conventional actions (e.g., other cities are raising taxes). Cities that cannot stop rationalizing their decisions and actions in such ways will alternate between unique and conventional manifestations of mediocrity.

One important lesson that I learned from working in local government is that there are no shortcuts. From a certain perspective, it appears attractive to use a city organization to build a local facility, organize a business improvement district, host a local event, sponsor a cultural exchange program, operate a senior center, etc. All these activities add something to the community when one focuses on the readily seen.

But in the name of simple and convenient local services, cities have created a complex disorder that jeopardizes all services. By forcing an array of local services into one service basket, city leaders relegate themselves to tough decisions. But city actions taken in support of residents and business owners should not be tough. It should not be tough for city officials to limit the use of city powers to the protection of residents and businesses. When I hear that a decision is tough, I know that the city is still trying to maximize local services and not maximize the freedom of its residents. And I know that the city is compelling someone in the community to pay for something they do not value or to give up something they do.

The truly smart, resilient, and progressive cities will challenge innovators nationwide to solve the problem of city infrastructure and local services. Such cities will do so not by creating new variations of their municipal monopoly franchises but by enabling *real* solutions for electricity, sewer, water, streets, parks, ambulance, etc. Some of these solutions will require changes to existing laws and regulations that deter private innovation in these areas.

Flourishing cities need the best from their residents, businesses, and nonprofit organizations. Such cities also need the best from their local governments. The personal, commercial, and governmental areas do not have to compete or conflict. On the contrary, these three areas are complementary. The residents and those who run noncommercial activities need the freedom to act and associate. Those who engage in commercial activities need the freedom to produce and trade. None of these areas require outside planning or control, but their agents need their decisions, actions, and property properly protected. This is something that only the local government can provide. And that government needs the moral authority to hold the local monopoly on force for these protective purposes.

Riding on our municipalities' many decisions are the livability of the local social and political environment and the efficacy of the institutions empowered to protect us all. If cities' pursuit of better times fixates on a fantasy future in which they discount the lessons of the past decades, they reinforce the policies that led to the current crisis. And if city officials allow better times to be defined in a manner that does not protect each resident's freedom to pursue a better life, they fail those residents.

But there is another option. City governments can enable genuine community—*community* whose flourishing emerges from the individual pursuits of residents who can act without the threat that others will use the authority of the city government to override their choices and impede their value pursuits.

Municipal leaders can unleash the innovation and creativity that their organizations have forcefully stifled for decades. *This* is what will save our city governments.

Fixing Municipal Budgeting

Municipalities have not made budgeting difficult. They have made it *impossible*. If we want to fix municipal budgeting, we need to recognize what local government is and what individual residents and business owners need—i.e., their fundamental human needs.

We need to discover the *value* of local government—local government that protects residents' freedom to engage in the activities they need to flourish. From there, municipal officials can deploy a local government that will enable such flourishing, and they can manage the delimited scope of activity that follows.

That is the first step in fixing municipal budgeting.

Bibliography

Associated Press. "Silverdome Sold to Canadian Company." November 23, 2009. Accessed, July 9, 2021, from https://espn.com/nfl/news/story?id=4683689.
Bastiat, Frédéric. "That Which Is Seen, and That Which Is Not Seen." Accessed June 18, 2021, from http://bastiat.org/en/twisatwins.html.
Carrington, Don. "Roanoke Rapids Finally Unloads Former Randy Parton Theatre." *Carolina Journal*, July 24, 2018. https://carolinajournal.com/news-article/roanoke-rapids-finally-unloads-former-randy-parton-theatre/.
City of Bend. "Vision, Mission and Values." Accessed June 8, 2021, from https://bendoregon.gov/government/departments/city-manager-s-office/vision-mission-and-values.
City of Glendale, CA. "Mission and Vision Statements." Accessed June 8, 2021, from https://glendaleca.gov/government/transparency/city-s-mission-vision-statement.
City of Paducah. "Mission, Vision, and Organizational Values." Accessed May 16, 2021, from http://paducahky.gov/mission-vision-and-organizational-values.
City of Sausalito. "City Council Approves Purchase of Bank of America Building." News from the City of Sausalito, August 21, 2020. https://sausalito.gov/Home/Components/News/News/4866/.
City of Walla Walla. "Statement of Mission, Vision & Values." Accessed June 8, 2021, from https://wallawallawa.gov/government/statement-of-mission-vision-values.
Committee for a Better New Orleans. "2018 People's Budget Report." Accessed May 20, 2021, from https://cbno.org/site/wp-content/uploads/2018-Peoples-Budget-Report.pdf.
Davidson, Kate. "Federal Covid-19 Aid Aims to Help Cities, States Avoid Cutting Jobs and Services." *The Wall Street Journal*, March 18, 2021. https://wsj.com/

M. Moses, *The Municipal Financial Crisis*,
https://doi.org/10.1007/978-3-030-87836-8

articles/federal-covid-19-aid-aims-to-help-cities-states-avoid-cutting-jobs-and-services-11616059802.

de Zwart, Frank. "Unintended but Not Unanticipated Consequences." *Theory and Society* 44, no. 3 (December 2015): 283–297. https://doi.org/10.1007/s11186-015-9247-6.

Fishlock, Diana. "If Prayer for Harrisburg Helps, Local Clergy Say 'Why Not?'" Penn Live, June 23, 2011. Accessed June 19, 2021, from https://pennlive.com/midstate/2011/06/if_prayer_for_the_health_of_ha.html.

Foltin, Craig. "Unrest in Government Accounting: GASB and the GFOA Square Off." *The CPA Journal*, March 2008. https://archives.cpajournal.com/printversions/cpaj/2008/308/p26.htm.

Gascón, George, and Todd Foglesong. "Making Policing More Affordable: Managing Costs and Measuring Value in Policing." Program in Criminal Justice Policy and Management, Harvard Kennedy School, December 2010. https://hks.harvard.edu/sites/default/files/centers/wiener/programs/pcj/files/NewPerspectivesPolicing-MakingPolicingMoreAffordable-Dec2010.pdf.

Glaeser, Edward L. *Triumph of the City: How Our Greatest Invention Makes Us Richer, Smarter, Greener, Healthier, and Happier*. New York: Penguin Books, 2012.

Government Finance Officers Association. "Achieving a Structurally Balanced Budget." Accessed May 16, 2021, from https://gfoa.org/materials/achieving-a-structurally-balanced-budget.

Government Finance Officers Association. "Financial Policies." Accessed May 20, 2021, from https://www.gfoa.org/materials/financial-policies-book.

Government Finance Officers Association. "Role of the Finance Officer in Supporting Fiscal Sustainability." Accessed May 18, 2021, from https://gfoa.org/materials/role-of-the-finance-officer-in-supporting-fiscal-sustainability.

Governmental Accounting Standards Board. "GASB Releases New Information That Will Significantly Change Financial Reporting by State and Local Governments." 1999.

Herbert, Auberon. *The Voluntaryist Creed*. Oxford: Oxford University Press, 1908.

Johnson, Jon, and Chris Fabian. "Priority Based Budgeting: Presentation of 'Resource Alignment Diagnostic Tool.'" Presentation at the City of Kalamazoo, Kalamazoo, MI, September 14, 2015. https://kalamazoocity.org/pbbdocuments/1301-center-for-priority-based-budgeting-rad-tool-presentation-september-14-2015-pdf/file.

Kavanagh, Shane. *The New Financial Sustainability Framework*. Chicago: Government Finance Officers Association, 2017. https://gfoaorg.cdn.prismic.io/gfoaorg/78f17413-bf27-4ce6-8d0b-64993c4776ba_Financial+Sustainability+White+Paper-v2_0.pdf.

Kavanagh, Shane. *Zero-Base Budgeting: Modern Experiences and Current Perspectives*. Chicago: Government Finance Officers Association, 2011. https://gfoa.org/materials/zero-base-budgeting.

Kavanagh, Shane, and Vincent Reitano. *Transparency: A Means to Improving Citizen Trust in Government*. Chicago: Government Finance Officers Association, 2018. https://gfoa.org/materials/transparency-a-means-to-improving-citizen-trust.

Kavanagh, Shane, Jon Johnson, and Chris Fabian. *Anatomy of a Priority-Driven Budget Process*. Chicago: Government Finance Officers Association, 2011. https://gfoa.org/materials/anatomy-of-a-priority-driven-budget-process.

Konisky, David M., and Manuel P. Teodoro. "When Governments Regulate Governments." *American Journal of Political Science* 60, no. 3 (2015): 559–574. https://doi.org/10.1111/ajps.12221.

Krinn, Keith L. "PRESIDENT'S MESSAGE: Lemonade in the New Normal." *Journal of Environmental Health* 73, no. 7 (2011): 4–8. Accessed May 20, 2021, from https://jstor.org/stable/26329175.

Krol, Robert, and Shirley Svorney. "The Collapse of a Noble Idea." *Regulation*, Winter 2004–2005, 30–33. https://cato.org/sites/cato.org/files/serials/files/regulation/2004/12/v27n4-3.pdf.

Malanga, Stephen. "Convention Wisdom." *City Journal*, Winter 2012. https://city-journal.org/html/convention-wisdom-13456.html.

Mullins, Daniel, John Mikesell, Chad Smith, Marvin Ward, and Chase Bricker. "Performance Budgeting / Budgeting for Results at the State Level." Presentation at the American Society for Public Administration, Washington, DC, March 18, 2014. https://slideshare.net/JMKamensky/aspa-performance-budgeting-32014-chad-smith.

National Advisory Council on State and Local Budgeting. *Recommended Budget Practices: A Framework for Improved State and Local Government Budgeting*. Chicago: Government Finance Officers Association, 1998. https://gfoaorg.cdn.prismic.io/gfoaorg/e4534548-fa06-47ad-9cc8-5f37e6e2f21e_RecommendedBudgetPractices.pdf.

Netter, Sarah. "Fire Departments Charge for Service, Asking Accident Victims to Pay Up." ABC News, February 3, 2010. Accessed June 10, 2021, from https://abcnews.go.com/Business/fire-department-bills-basic-services-horrify-residents-insurance/story?id=9736696.

Osborne, David, and Peter Hutchinson. *The Price of Government: Getting the Results We Need in an Age of Permanent Fiscal Crisis*. New York: Basic Books, 2004.

Osborne, David, and Ted Gaebler. *Reinventing Government: How the Entrepreneurial Spirit Is Transforming the Public Sector*. Reading: Addison-Wesley, 1992.

Public Banking Institute. "Legislation & Local Groups by State." Accessed June 10, 2021, from https://publicbankinginstitute.org/legislation-local-groups-by-state/.

Public Banking Institute. "Two Banking Models—Public and Private." Accessed June 10, 2021, from https://publicbankinginstitute.org/intro-to-public-banking/.

"Public Union Facts." Accessed May 16, 2021, from https://publicunionfacts.com/.

Ranson, WV. "City Council." Accessed June 8, 2021, from https://cityofransonwv.net/227/City-Council.

Ring, Edward. "California's Government Unions Collect An Estimated $800 Million Per Year." California Policy Center, July 13, 2018. https://californiapolic

ycenter.org/californias-major-government-unions-collect-over-800-million-per-year/.

Semuels, Alana. "The City That Gave Its Residents $3 Million." *The Atlantic*, November 6, 2014. https://www.theatlantic.com/business/archive/2014/11/the-city-that-gave-its-residents-3-million/382348/.

State of California. "California's Budget Process." Accessed May 20, 2021, from https://dof.ca.gov/budget/Budget_Process/.

US EPA. "Advancing Sustainable Materials Management: 2018 Fact Sheet." https://epa.gov/sites/production/files/2021-01/documents/2018_ff_fact_sheet_dec_2020_fnl_508.pdf.

Weber, Max. *From Max Weber: Essays in Sociology*. Translated by H. H. Gerth and C. W. Mills. New York: Oxford University Press, 1946.

Wheeler, Chris. "The Public Interest: We Know It's Important, but Do We Know What It Means." *AIAL Forum* 2, no. 48 (2006): 12–25.

Index

M. Moses, *The Municipal Financial Crisis*,
https://doi.org/10.1007/978-3-030-87836-8